THE AGELESS BODY

Chris Griscom

Light Institute Press

Cover design by Kokopelli Design, and Chris Griscom
Front cover photo by Teo Griscom
Back cover and inside photos by Megan Griscom
Drawings by Austin Hansen
Book design by Kokopelli Design

Library of Congress Cataloging-in-Publication Data
Griscom, Chris, 1942-
The Ageless Body
1. Light Institute of Galisteo (NM) 2. Griscom, Chris, 1942-
3. Nizhoni: The School for Global Consciousness 4. Spiritual healing
5. Health 6. New Age movement. I. Title
ISBN 0-9623696-1-6

Printed in the United States of America by Light Institute Press

The Ageless Body is dedicated
with great love and respect
to my own body
that has allowed me this magical life
and has shown me miracles
of its will and source

CONTENTS

Acknowledgements

My profound gratitude to the facilitators of the Light Institute who have encouraged and supported me through this creative venture.

My heart-filled thanks to my children; especially Teo and Bapu who have had to share me for so long with the book and to my daughter Megan for her wonderful photography. To Uli Schumacher for all her help arranging the details of its production. Thanks to Josef & Annie of Kokopelli Design for professionally editing and producing this book.

WORD TO THE READER

My friends,

This book about the **Ageless Body** is a little different than those I have written before. It incorporates many things I learned and taught years ago when my focus of work was directed to the functioning of the physical body. Writing this book offers me a completion of the circle whereby I have explored the body through it's bones and tissue and organs, through its feeling pathways and emotional storage processes, until I came upon its energy sources that not only provide it with growth and rejuvenation, but also with transcendence. Transcendence is the magical and divine quality of the body to meet any adversity and shift in such a way so as to survive or compensate by changing itself. It changes by altering its vibratory rate into a higher frequency which increases its energy levels and so transcends its former reality. By revisiting the age old knowings and bringing them to light in a format that is applicable to our modern pattern of life, we can begin to master our miraculous body and experience for ourselves the **Ageless Body** that is available through the wisdom hidden away by those who have dedicated their lives to practicing universal laws of matter. I know that whether you are eighteen or eighty, the message of this book applies to you and may well enhance the quality of your life. If you could realize that you alone have the power to design and motivate your own body, you will learn a tremendous amount about the meaning of life.

The body is not a solid, dense piece of matter that

grows, matures and dies. All of its expressions are party to the energies that move through it. We can become aware of these energies and influence them through our consciousness that provides everything in the universe. If we find the key to this consciousness, we will discover that our bodies are capable of feats of which we have not yet even dreamed!

The exploration of the **Ageless Body** centers around two points of reference concerning life. The search to live forever "young," and to live longer. To be perennially young concerns the expression of self, as well as issues related to the quality and purpose of life. We judge ourselves so strongly by how others see us that our attachment to the "outer wrapping" becomes a desperate struggle to elude time and seem ever available and desirable.

Living longer has undertones of the fear of dying and the hope of becoming immortal. As our human family evolves, we must see life and death in a different way in order to take advantage of the cosmic laws governing the process of embodiment. There is an interface between our physical energy on this plane and that same energy as it transcends this level of third dimensional existence and extends out into the universe. We are more than our physical existence. There is a conscious part of us that brings us into birth and carries us out from the body into worlds of pure energy, and back again. We must switch our search for life extension from avoidance of death to awareness of life.

Living longer is already within the grasp of modern technology. Technology can support and aid the body, but it cannot access the endless energy that sources life. It is the wisdom of the ancient masters that will provide the avenue for commanding **ageless bodies** full of energy and light. It is our turn to try their secrets so we can more fully use life, actively engaging in personal application of those universal laws that influence the amount of vital energy available to our bodies.

Perhaps it is my deep commitment to learning these universal secrets that has brought me to "death's door" six times in this lifetime. I have left the body through accident, through illness, and then returned. Each time I learned more about what is beyond the physical body and what is controlling it.

Each of my near-death experiences has taught me different aspects of the laws which govern life, and most profoundly, the unwavering experience that we exist beyond our bodies! This consciousness, which is not entrapped within the body, can and does select for us our life experiences on multiple levels. The motive for this book came from a very powerful death experience I had in 1988 which so altered my physical body that I realized I would have to actually "work" my body back into a healthy state, lest I fall prey to the syndrome of chronic illness. After the shock of the death experience, my body immediately passed through menopause and began taking on all the signs of rapid aging.

The episode occurred during a trip to Mexico when I needed some stitching of a wound. Though I warned the doctors that I was allergic to most of the analgesic drugs, they intravenously administered an anesthesia that caused my heart and breathing to stop. My consciousness underwent the most fantastic energetic explosions as it pulled up and out of my body and entered into a dimension of light which is infinitely beyond what we experience in our normal awareness.

Meanwhile, my body lay lifeless on the operating table an entire hour while the surgeons waited for my return. Though they were able to reinstate my breathing, there was apparently "permanent" damage to the left ventricle of my heart. The heart specialist suggested that I would need a by-pass. To make matters worse, I also came down with typhoid fever three days later after being given some unpurified water.

As often happens during episodes of profound illness, a strange clarity or expansion of awareness took over my consciousness. I could perceive my perfect body as distinct from the one lying on the bed. Guided by this clarity, I called upon my etheric body of light, and superimposed the heart of my light body onto my damaged physical heart so as to re-imprint the structure of that heart. Within three days the doctors were shaking their heads and saying, "This can't be! We have now a different electrocardiograph reading and that is impossible!" But it was possible because I had tapped into the light energy which holds the blueprint of the physical body and merged it into my physical cells, exciting them to create something completely new. It is a physical body that is being helped through its connection to the universal energy of the life force. Because of it, I am very much alive!

After I returned to the United States, I went to see my friend Alex Orbito, the famous Philippine psychic surgeon. Alex worked twice on my heart to remove the scar tissue, after which I was able to go on the lecture tours I had scheduled just 10 days after this all occurred.

Nevertheless, the aging process had taken hold in a discouraging way. It was as if the body had become infected with the imprint of dying and I realized that I would have to do something to alter my body's interpretation of its own timetable of life. This book is the result of my re-aquaintance with the many teachings I have come across in terms of the body and its habit of aging.

Though **The Ageless Body** is full of tips and processes to help you become aware of how to influence your body, I hope most of all that you will realize the absolute power you have to affect your experience in the body through your **consciousness.** It is the attention and communication you share with your body that makes such a great difference.

The exercises I will demonstrate for you have had a profound effect on my own body. One of the first things that happened when I began to do them regularly is that the pulses of my internal organs changed dramatically. In Chinese medicine, we take the pulses of the twelve internal organs which give a reading of the body in concert with itself. Each of the twelve internal organs has a rhythm or pulse that expresses its energetic state at any moment.

Since this last of my near-death experiences, I have had only a faint and irregular heart pulse. The pericardial pulse was, for practical purposes, non-existent. All through my life I have had light, "wiry" pulses because my focus in physical form has been, at the very least, tenuous. Within weeks of doing these exercises, I began to have a strong regular pulse in all the organs, including the kidney pulse, which usually is diminished at my age. This is indisputable proof to me that something beyond body chemistry is going on. The effect of these exercises have produced miracles for so many people, I simply felt this had to be shared with everyone.

Come with me on this journey into your body and your consciousness, to uncover and dissolve old thought forms you have had about aging and self-identity. You will discover how absolutely amazing you are, and hopefully, you will try some of these fabulous exercises that have been tested throughout the centuries by sentient beings who actually lived extended and purposeful lives.

Ultimately, the **Ageless Body** is a vehicle of fantastic wealth and complexity that was designed by divine power for you and me to experience a sojourn here on the material plane. As you learn about its interweaving subtle energies, you will begin to fathom what death has taught me: all that is real in the universe need not be seen or touched to still influence reality. The **Ageless Body** is not a new scientific discovery, it is an awakening of what has always been there, but has never been explored.

INTRODUCTION

In today's hard-driving world, the pursuit of fame and fortune is only superseded by the pursuit of timeless youth. While on the one hand we do not value the contributions nor make space for the young in our world, we worship their bodies and their energy. Youthful vigor is a message we all want to communicate to the world because we feel we must appear to be full of power so that someone else will not take our spot in the fickle marketplace of life.

This very concept of buying and selling entraps us within a fixed and limited expression of existence in which the outside world hoards too much of our freedom. Frozen to our spot, we await the approval and judgement of others. As we search our bag of tricks to sway others, it is the body that often offers us the most sure avenue of approval. Almost everybody needs love and can be lured by physical attention. Thus, we count on our body to offer that attention and hope to receive some in return. Unfortunately, as we grow older, this body crutch deserts us and we suffer anxiety that we will no longer be chosen and appreciated physically. To avoid the inevitable situation, we delude ourselves with all manner of deception about age and employ absolutely any devise we can to hide the tell-tale signs of aging. All of us recall the myth of Peter Pan who refused to grow up.

In the innocence of our childhood, we plead and dream of being bigger and older than we are because we presume that the wielding of power comes only with "bigness" of bodies and the experience of the world. As the rush of puberty wears off, there is a slow dawning of realization that once we are bigger, much will be required of us. The security that someone will help us and that everything will be okay begins to wane as we take our first peeks into the reality of the adult world. Here begins an inner struggle in which the body rushes ahead to fulfill its destiny and the mind begins to stall as it grasps the panorama of possible futures. In our hearts whisper secret thoughts, longings for the comfort of childhood!

Initially the body and its thrust of energy carry us along into the river of life. As each stage of adulthood casts a heavier and heavier cloak over our once lighthearted self-image, we begin to reminisce with nostalgia about the "glamour of youth." We constantly replay exciting adventures of our high school or college days because we no longer dare to embark upon such episodes now, lest someone think us ridiculous or lacking in seriousness. As life deposits itself in the sediment of goals and tasks, we begin a dangerous tendency of devaluing ourselves and enshrining youth as the lost haven of hope.

As we cast our scrutinizing attention upon the screen of success and failure, the score mounts highest for efforts which involve that free-floating energy of enthusiasm and sheer activity so readily available in youth. Especially in hindsight, the events of our youthful years echo the lost happiness of the "good old days" which seem so much brighter than the oppression of the present. As young people, we dare so much because we are restless for action and capable of sudden bursts of high voltage energy. We identify with our bodies and use them extensively in our myriad pursuits. The accomplishments of our careers are still unripened in youth, while the pursuit of love and company absorb our attention.

Why should this end? Why do we surrender the light-hearted trust in life that helps us to fearlessly embrace any new possibility? If only we could focus on the wisdom we gain as we move through life, our bodies would be able to express a grace and dignity that is not available to the more scattered energy of the young.

As we travel on the path of life, our judgement of ourselves and others wears away the veneer of untouchability until we erroneously conclude that we cannot win at life. We have so many thought-forms about the aging process, the very negativity of which actually cause it to occur. In this book, **The Ageless Body**, you will see that what you think or believe, creates form and becomes entrapped within the physical body. This is how you literally think yourself into helplessness and ultimately, your death.

It need not be that way. You can gain mastery over your body and maintain it in a timeless, **ageless** state. If you have grown old and stale in your mind or your body, you can most likely alter this condition by the power of your intent and the simple teachings set forth in this book. The **Ageless Body** is not a body that is forever pickled in the wrinkle-less, fat-less mannequin of youth. It is a body that is not old because it functions in health, performs its physical tasks at the command of the consciousness, and therefore becomes truly **ageless** because it is in total harmony with its relationship to life!

DISCOVERING THE
AGELESS BODY

"We are not just bones and blood and flesh, we are magnificent conduits of energy that make us laugh and dance and live!"

The search for the secrets of youth and **The Ageless Body** are not the passion of the modern generation alone, they have consumed the thoughts and efforts of humans since the dawn of time. Every great civilization has experimented with some formula or technique to hide the mirror of age and decrepitude. Today the fruit of our learning has altered the generational landscape such that populations on every continent are averaging higher and higher mean age as the advancement of modern technology so expertly stays the execution of death. With heroic measures such as new hearts, kidneys, and everything from hair transplants to hips, knees and blood, life goes on more comfortably and longer. Through the application of biochemistry and advanced pharmaceuticals, we can slow or compensate somewhat for the degeneration of the body.

Still, there is no medical cure for aging and its ravaging effect on the body. While searching for the key to aging, scientists around the world are exploring the intricacies of genetics, the interplay of environmental factors, nutrition and exercise. Nevertheless, technology has thus far served us only as the handyman who fixes the damage temporarily with what is available, or experiments with the mechanics of bodily function without enough recognition of what actually causes it all to happen. One of the interesting theories about the aging process is the tentative discovery of a "death hormone" which is activated at puberty and begins the seemingly inevitable progression towards death.

Happily, new discoveries in the fields of molecular science, nutrition and biochemistry are offering us a peep through the threshold of bodily complexity into the fantastic world of living engineering that orchestrates the human vehicle. However, we will never crack the cosmic secrets of life until we go beyond the physical or even biochemical processes, and into the source of energy itself, which is our "true" body.

We have done little to discover our true bodies, yet we require endless energy from them and we give so much neglect that it is a wonder they function at all. While we have looked for all manner of quick fixes, pills, substances and techniques to make our bodies young or different, the great cosmic giggle is that the essential force of life occurs within and beyond the body. We are not just bones and blood and flesh, we are magnificent conduits of energy that make us laugh and dance and live! If we are to find the secret of the **Ageless Body**, we must look beyond the physical, material level and into the octaves of pure energy which is the stuff that provides the "juice" for our bodies. The ancients have known for thousands of years that aging is not a foregone conclusion and that it can be influenced by working with the special energies of the body. Though the body naturally matures, it never need go from maturity to decrepitude.

The mystery of the body remains entrapped in the unfathomable question of where life itself comes from. What is it that sparks the fire of life into existence? Is it some kind of omnipotent energy that courses through all that exists? The ancient sages all spoke about this life force energy that interpenetrates matter, and through its presence, sparks the flame of life.

One of the major tenets of this book is that the healthy body is an **Ageless Body** because the rhythm of its life energy is constantly being rejuvenated and regenerated so that it endlessly continues its potential. How might we know that there is a potential in the body to continue on without aging and deterioration? Perhaps only because it has been spoken of for eons of time. There have been masters and ordinary people who have lived hundreds of years, showing proof that there is another way. As long as there is even a myth, or one person who has achieved such an incredible feat, it will be the dream of all humanity to attempt that personal and yet collective feat. Through the vast reaches of psyche and genetic patterns, the whisper of ageless actuality will continue to prick our awareness. We must eternally strive towards that timeless state, because the body knows deep within its essence that this is a choice.

How can you discover your **Ageless Body**? The first thing is to become aware of the body as it is. Mostly you probably only think of your body when it hurts. You notice it when your back is stiff, or you can't seem to move as fast as you once did, or you feel heavy and have trouble digesting. You must learn to treat it like someone special you live with, because of course, you do. When was the last time you said "thank you" to your body or acknowledged it for doing something wonderful for you? It is easy to treat it like family, as if the "thank you's" and loving kindness didn't apply because of the familiarity. If, instead of complaining to your body about what it won't do, you spoke to it with encouragement, you would be surprised at the immediate response. If you discover the areas that need strengthening, you can set to work on your first miracles.

Begin by really taking a good look at your body and evaluating what you think is true of it. You know whether you are a good runner or get out of breath quickly. You know if you metabolize slowly by the weight on your body, whether you can digest easily, or often experience gas. You are aware of your sex drive, your capacity to get up in the morning and go all day. Perhaps you know what kind of strengths or weaknesses you have in terms of the organs of your body-- if you tend towards lung or bladder infections, or have a strong heart. You can start by assessing your body. This isn't a question of what someone else has told you, it's what you know about your body yourself because you live in it and can truly feel how it is. You might even choose to make a list for yourself of your strong and weak points, as you perceive them consciously or mentally. Of course, each thought-form you have about your body is a prophecy waiting to be fulfilled. If you leave your body unattended with a negative conclusion, it will echo that thought-form to the cellular level until it is so deeply entrenched that the body will think that it is the way it is supposed to be.

Once you identify what needs to be healed, you must get to work to change it. Most likely, you are much too critical about your body, and your evaluation of it will give little credit to your recognition of what a magnificent and powerful thing it is. It is such a futile hope that you can turn your body over to an outside source and stand back while somebody else fixes it. You are the only expert designer of your physical vehicle, and only through your consciousness can what you have created be changed.

If you begin to praise your body for its health and stamina, it will reward you by demonstrating its power. There is nothing about your body that can't be brought into balance, since homeostasis is the major goal of all the parts working to maintain the whole. You can help greatly by coming to know your body on an intimate level.

Very few people are in touch on deep levels with their bodies. For example, are you aware of your kidneys, pineal gland or gall bladder? It might seem overwhelming to try to learn about your body from a medical or scientific point of view because the body of knowledge is so vast. But there is a simple way you can get to know what is happening in your body. I call it scanning.

SCANNING

Scanning is a technique of exploring your body that focuses on a different level of perception, rather than thought forms. Scanning allows you to glance at your body from an energetic point of view and teaches you a new kind of relationship whereby the body can show you what it wants you to know. By scanning the body, you can see the various areas that need strengthening and loving. It has been done in many ways throughout the centuries.

Here is how to do it: Close your eyes and ask your body to appear before you just as if you were looking in the mirror. You know what your naked body looks like. Put that body before your minds' eye. Then, imagine that you are a scanning machine and glance down from your head to your feet. As you glance, give your body the mandate that any areas that need attention will flash to you or show themselves as dark spots. Even if you see a dark spot, continue down to your feet and then back up to your head. Once you have been shown the various dark spots, you will be able to change them with the techniques I will show you in this book.

Years ago I taught the children in my school how to scan the body of strangers, as did the famous psychic Edgar Cayce. I would ask them to lay down on the floor, close their eyes and imagine the body of the person whose name I gave them. The younger ones would wiggle around and peek out the window, so much so that the first time I thought they simply could not do such a complicated exercise. What a great shock it was for me when I asked them what they saw and they all reported exactly the area of the body that was affected. Though they did not know the names of the organs or parts, they would identify exactly that place in the body as a dark spot or red fire!

You can do this same exercise to discover the strong, healthy parts of your body. Sometimes this information is a great surprise and can do wonders to help you change negative impressions about yourself. It is so easy to develop fears about your body's health. Feeling safe in your body is of utmost importance in attaining the **Ageless Body.** If you are in a constant state of anxiety about your physical body, it will grow old from the stress of endless alert that does not allow it to recuperate from the siege of negative attention.

When you do this kind of exercise to discover your strong points, you may feel deeply comforted by the reassurance that you are okay. If in your scanning, for example, you discover that your lungs are just fine, you may relax your level of anxiety, thus helping you to digest better and subsequently feel more energetic because your relaxation increases the absorption of nourishment.

The more strong points you discover in your body, the more **Ageless** you will become because your sense of yourself will be one of vitality and health. The agelessness of the body is really about how well it functions. And as you realize all the fantastic things it can do for you, your ability to trust in your body will save you from the anxieties which are, themselves, one of the major sources of ill-health. Because you expose it to the elements -- sun, pollution, and stress -- its journey will be reflected upon your skin and organs, but it will adapt and continue its never-ending process of existence. The body learns to become expedient and very efficient with its flow of energy; it is a wonderful and intelligent wizard of compensation. At forty-five years you may feel the exuberance of a "staying power" that allows you to out-distance earlier attempts of years gone by because your body has become expedient with its energy and knows how to release a steady stream that can carry you through, just as well or better than the quick bursts you experienced in your youth. I remember the fascination I had when nursing my children, as in each nursing era my body wasted less and less milk from excitement or overreaction to demand. There was always plenty of milk and each baby was as chubby as the last, without milk always staining my clothes. My body simply grew better and better at measuring the need and balancing the output. In a thousand ways our bodies learn to expend energy with reference to the whole.

Energy levels in the body are definitely an important criteria for agelessness. I have seen many people in the Andes that cluster around one hundred years of age and yet could climb the mountain every day and find the energy to take care of all their tasks. Exploring where and how the body generates this fantastic energy of life is indeed worthy of our time and attention. To seek the source of all this energy, we must come to know our bodies in a new way, an energetic way. Ultimately, we will have to ponder life's mysteries from its true source, which is divine.

THE SOURCE OF BODILY ENERGY

There is more than one kind of energy utilized by the body. First there is an electromagnetic energy that pervades all the energy systems. Every synoptic spark is carried by an electric charge. Whether you are thinking, moving or sleeping, electrical currents are coursing through you, providing you with the energy you need. The food you eat gives you a source of energy which your body assimilates by breaking down the crude substances into smaller particles and storing or releasing them as it determines appropriate. The air you breathe brings you oxygen molecules of pure energy that give life to all your cells. The magnificent biochemistry of your body creates thousands of enzymatic and catalytic reactions that fuel the fire of unquenchable life. Yet, what actually sparks that fire is still a mystery to us all.

We have whole systems of energy in and around the body that provide us with a glimmer of our vast energy potential. There are nerve channels that carry messages of action from the brain to the muscles and back again. There are meridian channels that carry a mysterious, electrical energy the Chinese call Chi. Several thousand years before technology could attest to the presence of energy meridians, these channels and their energy points were utilized with breathtaking accuracy to stimulate and balance the flows of life within and around the body by the ancient healing societies of the Far East. The Chi was said to follow the blood, to give it life force energy and then the blood would follow the Chi in a never-ending circuitry of currents whose strength determined the length and quality of one's life.

The tiny energy points on the meridians can be stimulated by needles to increase, decrease or harmonize the energies coursing inside each point with the rest of the body as a whole. This system of energetics is called acupuncture and is finding increasing popularity as we become aware of and practice its great laws of energy coherence. The points on the meridians are fed by huge energy centers of spinning light called chakras.

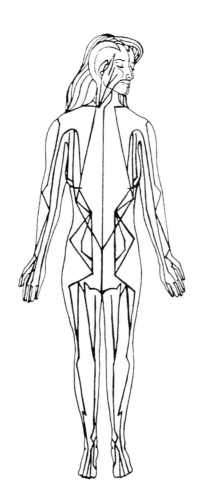

Energy Meridians

The chakras are vortexes of highly charged energy that feed the body at its source. They create a cohesive field of fast-spinning energy around and through the body. This is the famous "auric field" known to the ancients and rediscovered as technology has finally constructed instruments sensitive enough to detect it. The auric field emanates out from the body radiating the chakric energy that expresses the quality of life force each of us is carrying. Though there are seven major chakric centers rising from the base of the trunk up to the top of the head, there are also many minor ones on the extremities such as the shoulders, elbows, knees, wrists and ankles, feet and hands, as well as two that extend above the head. The major chakras spark the endocrine system that performs as a threshold between subtle energy forces and those we recognize as pertaining to our body. Many of the exercises in this book will be directed to stimulating and increasing the energy of the chakras. Throughout the eons, those who were masters of their bodies were aware of these spinning chakras and knew how to strengthen and balance them. You and I can do the same and experience the incredible increase of energy that comes when our chakras are open and radiating.

When people age, there is a general decline of energy throughout their bodies as the once exuberant energy field becomes laden with emotional and physical debris. The thoughts and joints become weighted by virtual crystals of inert materials, both mineral and emotional deposits, that stop the range of motion in the limbs and the mind!

All the systems of the body are reflected in the energy field, and if even one is out of balance, there will be a corresponding weakness or dysfunction in others because they are all connected. This is why you learn so much by scanning your body and can feel the powerful changes that take place by focusing on any part of your energy field.

If you could survey the interrelated systems of your body, you would see that any change on one level will ultimately effect changes on other levels. For example, the expression of your body on outer, more physical or muscular levels, will indeed create an effect on inner organ levels. There is definitely a dance of relationship between the internal organs and the outer body. If the great muscle of the heart is weak, you can expect that the other muscles will not be particularly strong either, since the heart feeds the muscles. So too, if the chakras are spinning slowly and discordantly, the endocrines will be unable to stoke the fires of the organs that control the body's functioning.

You do not have to have any special talents to balance your chakras, meridians, auric field or even internal organs.

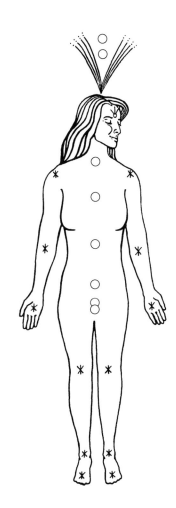

Chakra System

All you need is the willingness to listen to your body and come to know it as it is, while learning to command it to perform on a timeless, universal energy level to which it is always connected. It is a wondrous adventure to contemplate the effects of altering bodily energy at its source. Something drives this energy into body. It is a divine spark that sets you on your way. It does not abandon you to aging and dying, rather, it accompanies you through all the great lessons of your life until your internal "soul" clock calls you home. Life can be a drudgery if one forgets that it is ourselves who have orchestrated the master blueprint to include all the experiences necessary for our soul's growth. We needn't become crystallized by these learning experiences if we could remember what we are doing, and why. Only because we do forget, do we become so heavy with negativity and all manner of poisons that our own bodies cannot withstand us.

Rarely will you see a truly happy person who is sick, or someone who nurtures their physical body age early. This is because the lessons offered by illness, usually unconditional love and patience, are not heeded. A body that is nurtured and loved for its gift of life, will not betray its keeper. Illness should never be considered a punishment or a weakness however, for it is always the body giving us a profound teaching that could be learned in no other way. Only the critical illnesses I endured have taught me great truths about myself and my body: one of the most important of these, is that anything can be changed.

When you begin to feel the weight of life's chores over you, you may see its cloak as a pretext for feeling that you cannot succeed. If you fall into the habit of using your body as an excuse, it will manifest those excuses in real terms. It is the decline of your will to live, that dims the challenge from your eyes, and the spring from your step. You can regain that will to live as you become aware of life as a "passage." Discovery of your **Ageless Body** will help free you from the alarm of an incessantly ticking clock of life, and give you the grace to enjoy its gifts in an endless present. The lightness and energy that is really you can be contacted and set in motion to model and influence your physical body. You can improve your vitality and your radiance by discovering how to wield your life force as your body learns to take its cues from these more subtle, yet powerful energies.

COMMUNING WITH YOUR BODY

"Communication with your body can become an art so refined and powerful as to actually enter into the realm of communion within which you and your body merge in an exquisite way."

When your body speaks to you through its energy and its love, there begins a true communion that brings you into connection with something sacred. Your body is truly your best friend: a friend that loves you beyond all judgement, a friend that will do anything for you, and that provides you with an opportunity to experience the sacred pulse of life. If you learn to commune with your body, much of the aloneness and sense of separation will be lifted from your life. It has been with you from the beginning and can remind you of joys and secrets you have long since forgotten. The devotedness of your body will help you climb any mountain, dance into the night, and even to be so still in its consciousness that you may discover your own deepest self.

If you aspire to be **Ageless**, you must learn to joke and play with your body and become actual friends with it. The miracle of **ageless**ness depends on a convergence of conscious energy that dissolves blockages and promotes a free-flowing exchange so that your body can rejuvenate itself as it was designed. If you develop a trusting relationship with your body, it will follow your wishes, and in so doing, you will know that you need not fear bodily imbalances that lead to disease, or a body that doesn't work for you.

We are all too afraid of our bodies. We treat them as if they were a foreign advisory whose language we do not speak. Not only must we get over this fear, but we must learn how to commune and command the body. We expect it to sabotage us and we fearfully ask professional strangers to tell us what is the matter with our bodies when we could not possibly be separate from the cause of any ailment that occurs inside us. It is ourselves who live within the walls and confines of the body and are privy to everything that goes on inside and around it. Somewhere along the line we have lost our ability to communicate with our bodies. We have cornered ourselves in the limited mind and forgotten this primary language so crucial to our healthy experience of life. In our isolation from the body, we have become afraid and alienated from ourselves. Fear is a major pathway of destruction. FEAR IS THE ONLY DISEASE, and fear kills!

In our family, we have a house rule of not being sick longer than 24 hours. Whenever a child is sick, we always have a conversation with the body to find out what it is trying to tell us and what it wants. Then we set about giving it what it is seeking. With the first symptom, outside activity is stopped and full attention is placed on what the body needs. No school, job, date or other function takes precedent over the body. Sometimes it is a color, certain foods or substances, and even emotional expression that is called for. Throughout the raising of six children, I have always been quietly astounded when a sore throat or fever, as well as other more distressing symptoms, obediently disappear within the allotted time. Of course, I am fully aware of how this teaches young ones that being sick is not as fun as being healthy and so they rapidly become vigilantes of their bodies, lest they miss out on life!

Being funny or playful with our bodies seems much more difficult as we get older because of the illusion that formality is a necessary aspect of authority. The body is only interested in clear communication and it will respect you just as much through a little silliness. Think of the way you were with your body as a kid. You healed so quickly, not only because children rebound faster, but because you had a different sense of time and were innocent of the laws of probability that limit the freedom of consciousness. If you told your body it absolutely could jump over the fence, then you could. You could make it spin around a long time before you allowed yourself to fall down in dizziness. If you promised yourself you could swim to the end of the pool, you did. These are the same things you can continue to do now. The goals may be different, or similar. Perhaps you want to run that five miles, or lose five pounds. If you pledge your body with the same trusting fervor you did then, the results will be the same.

You must engage with your body as if it were a real person; encourage it, love it, tell it what you need. Do you ever talk to yourself in the mirror? Do you ever hug yourself out of pure glee? Try the language of the five senses that are so beloved to your body. Touch, sight, smell, sound, taste are all elementary and yet wonderful ways to please and communicate with your body. They are a part of the language system set up by the body with corresponding sensory organs to channel and organize each perception. Through the main five, as well as the "sixth" or psychic sense, you can experience explicit exchanges with your body that bring you great pleasure as well as crucial information about your internal and external environments.

In truth, there are more than seventy senses with which to perceive and communicate. You have five senses of radiation alone: sight, visibility or invisibility, radiation, temperature and electromagnetic frequencies. These seventy senses are taught at the Nizhoni School for Global Consciousness where students learn to perceive radiation and other subtle energies that impinge upon the body. As you discover the seventy senses, you will begin a new octave of consciousness in which **ageless**, timeless realities move in a sea of creative perception.

THE LANGUAGE OF TOUCH

Your body is extremely sensitized to touch. It was one of the first imprints of being loved and protected that you recorded on a bodily level. Though it was someone else who caressed you then, you should realize that it would be a great gift to your Emotional Body to know that now you can fulfill your own needs of security. You do not have to wait for someone else to touch you for the pleasure of the experience. You can stroke or pat yourself with just as much delight. In fact, your body would probably prefer you to touch it since you know exactly how much pressure or speed is best. What is fantastic is that you can simultaneously receive and give the touch.

All too often we are too self-conscious to touch ourselves, as if sensuality were inextricably connected to sexual intention and therefore must be delegated to someone outside ourselves. Indelibly, you were taught very young that this kind of self-engaging activity is wrong, or at least not appropriate. All the emphasis on outside approval and validation has created a world of fearful, lonely people who feel totally helpless by themselves. If you feel like rubbing yourself, whether for pleasure or to ease an ache, your body will take heed of your touch as a message of caring and a command to let go of the congestion that is causing pain. Go ahead and do it.

THE LANGUAGE OF SIGHT

This is the language most utilized by us with our bodies because we use sight as a principle indicator of reality. We trust and depend upon our visual acuity to guide us through life. We can look in the mirror and measure our age. This may be a big drawback to **agelessness** because it binds age on a continuum of youth to antiquity. If you notice your wrinkles growing deeper, or your hair turning grey, you may begin to despair that aging and all its attending disabilities are about to overcome you. In one sense the mirror is lying to you because it shows only the rather fixed exterior of your being. Rarely will you behold the expression of wisdom in your eyes through the mirror, or a spontaneous delight that spreads over you, or the spark that "knowing" brings as you converge your awareness upon a concept or deed.

When you look into the mirror, look at what your body is communicating to you. If you have circles under your eyes in the morning, you need to find out if you are sleeping too little or too much, and whether you are drinking too much coffee, which is a main contributor to dark areas under the eye. Your body is telling you these things, all you have to do is ask for confirmation. How? Just sit quietly and ask. "Should I sleep more?" You will get an answer; usually as a feeling or even in words!

Don't look for the negative, look for the positive. Visualize how you want to look and see that in "action." Perhaps you feel fat. Don't look for the fat as if you were frozen in a photo. Watch yourself move and see how much better you look when you see yourself as a flowing, alive person. As you move, the weight looks much different because it is more a part of you rather than something you are just carrying in excess. It is how you move that creates an impression of **ageless**ness. I have seen very chubby people who move like dancers, can do the splits and are so fluid that I never think of them as carrying around the burden of fat. I have also seen very thin people who move so stiffly that I always think them much older than they are because their bodies are definitely too heavy for them.

THE LANGUAGE OF SOUND

Sound is one of the most important ways of communing with your body. As you listen to a special music or tone that you like, you have the opportunity to tell your body about yourself on a vibrational level. Your body will attune itself to you through the sound. Because of this alignment effect of sound, it is truly one of the most powerful tools for balancing and healing the body. By the same token, sound can be an incredibly destructive energy, and you must pay attention to the sounds around you and observe how they affect your mood and your sense of well being. If they are in discord with your vibration, they can quicken the deterioration of your cells through their stress-provoking effect. This is as true for the five-year old child as the fifty-year old adult.

Sound preferences have always been said to amplify the generational gap. The volume teenagers can tolerate is probably directly related to the high pitch of their powerfully pulsing cells. This same pitch is indubitably too much for the cells of older people. However, it is often the low noise vibrations that can most disrupt the body's natural rhythm. The hum of fans, vents, computers and other machines can throw the body completely off its pulse. The worst thing about these "white" sounds is that your ear gets used to them and they go unnoticed. Whenever you enter a space where you will spend a good deal of your time, it is important to stop and notice the sounds in that space and ask your body if any of them need to be neutralized. If so, give your body a mental command that it will not be affected by these noises: "My body will not focus on or be disturbed by these sounds." You will be amazed at how efficiently you and your body can work together to lower the stress levels brought on by annoying environmental energies.

Use sound to energize or relax your body. There is nothing new in this except how expertly you can accomplish it with your conscious intention. Today there are many sound choices to help you attune your body. There are sounds of nature such as those of rainforest, waves and thunder; sounds of higher vibrations like dolphin and whale voices, bells and mantric chants. For babies and children there are the sounds of human heartbeats. Some parents are using sounds pressed to the womb to teach children math and science before they are born. Although there is some evidence that fetuses can record and subsequently relate to these imprints, it is probably not a good idea in the light of individual response to vibrations.

What good is it to override a genetic or spiritual necessity to learn the arts by forcefully pre-programing mathematics, for example, when to do so may create a mathematician who is always caught between the head and the heart? He may have a haunting feeling that there is something missing, and therefore place no value or joy on the skill which was thrust upon him before birth, to please a need of the parents. It is really a form of psychic manipulation that can bring confusion and a vague sense of incompleteness.

THE LANGUAGE OF SMELL

The sense of smell directs your attention to the world around you. There are more than ten thousand different odors that give you cues and form memories about your experiences in life. They identify your lovers, places you have been, and your health. Smell helps you perceive who is who in social and business interactions. Through smell you can decipher if someone is confident or afraid, and even whether they are available on sexual or friendly levels.

Though you are intimately aware of your own bodily smells, you may not have ever thought of what those smells are in terms of your body talking to you. It would be very helpful to begin to notice your body odors, not from the point of view of sociability, but from recognition of bodily function. For example, smell yourself and see what kinds of smells come from you in the morning and in the night when you go to bed. Can you smell the pollution that sticks to your clothes and hair? Notice if your underarm smells are stronger on one side of your body. This would indicate that your yin/yang balance is a little off. If it is stronger on your right side, I would recommend that you take liver tinctures to strengthen your liver which is a major organ of detoxification. You may want to "flush" your liver to clear it of congestion. Here is an old formula used in many parts of the world for just this purpose:

1 Tbls. cold pressed olive oil

Juice of one lemon

A pinch of cayenne pepper

Mix ingredients and drink first thing in the morning. The effect of this is to jolt the gallbladder which then flushes the liver. You may feel nothing in which case you can go ahead and have breakfast. Usually, the flush will make you empty your bowel. If you feel a little nauseated, just add some apple juice or water to dilute the mixture and lie down for about five minutes before going on. If this is too strong for you, simply cut the portions in half. Ask your body how often you should take a liver flush. You will be amazed at how it changes the way your body smells and especially how it changes your breath.

The odor of your breath is an excellent indicator of your overall health and vitality. The ancient Chinese doctors would always smell the skin around the bellybutton and the breath to ascertain the condition of a patient. If the stomach is not digesting properly, the toxic effect of putrification will always back up and be present in the mouth. Mouthwashes are not the answer to bad breath. You must work on your diet and digestion. I can smell a meat eater across the room because of strong odor and I'm sure this is one of the major factors in our frightening scent to wild animals who easily detect our presence.

Check to see that your body does not smell stale. The stale smell is a reflection of an aging body. If there is energy passing through the body and the internal tides are flowing, you will have a vibrant smell unique to you. If you don't like the smell of your body, change it from the inside by altering your daily routine. Through exercises and breath work, as well as a new diet, you will very soon smell differently.

Some people can't smell much. This is another side-effect of aging as the body's ability to produce B vitamins decreases. Your emotional state, diet and hereditary factors also contribute to your capacity to smell. The neurons in the nose are replaced every thirty days, however, so you can begin to focus your attention on this most magnificent of our senses to improve your delight. Take your body on a smelling tour and simply attune yourself to the odors around you. One way to enrich the pleasure of being in body is to seek out smells that trigger joy in you. Is it the smell of chocolate chip cookies coming out of the oven, freshly cut grass, perfume, the ocean, the smell of a new car? Each of us has an almost inexhaustible repertoire of smells that have meaning to us, that remind us or alter our reality enough to bring us a special experience.

I have a delicately intuitive olfactory sense that is very helpful in my life. When I worked in the National Penitentiary of Bolivia, the inmates affectionately called me "the nose" because I could tell almost everything they had been doing and when, by how they smelled. Like the proverbial hound dog, I knew which drugs and at what time they had indulged.

During the multi-incarnational sessions at the Light Institute, I have been jolted more than once as the scenes being re-lived by a client emerge not only in technicolor, but with full olfactory recall. Suddenly the room will smell of a hospital just milliseconds before the person describes it. The musky wet smell of a forest, the perfume of a French sitting room, the indelible smell of fear that exposes what could otherwise be disguised: all of these reinforce the body's attempt to communicate what is truly real. When we review a life to decipher its themes, it is imperative to clear from the mind of the cell all the debris left by its olfactory memory. Otherwise, when you smell that smell again, your Emotional Body will use it to rebound and repeat as close as possible that which it has known before.

Ferdinand the Bull has nothing over on me as I too, can pass hours in the pursuit of smell. If I need to lift my spirits, I will go into greenhouses and prowl around until I find plants that thrill my nose. I always emerge rejuvenated and refreshed, ready for the next round. Although the source of attraction to a particular odor may be rooted in past memory, it is distinctly a faculty of communication you can use to stimulate your body now, thus giving it "reason" to live on and to risk the future. The comfort of seasonal smells remind one that life goes on and that each time zone, day or night, spring or fall, will offer a structure of familiarity upon which you can base a thousand new and wonderful variations to your **Ageless** awareness.

THE LANGUAGE OF TASTE

Taste is very closely related to smell. You will certainly recognize how the mouth waters when you smell a delicious food that you adore. The taste buds on your tongue help you link up your association between a familiar smell and its quality of taste. You can distinguish between sweet, sour, salty and bitter. The sweet taste buds are on the tip of your tongue offering an initial delight. The salty and sour are on the sides of the tongue, and the bitter is at the back. Often when the stomach is off balance, you will taste a metallic or bitter taste at the back of the throat. Sometimes you may feel a craving for one or another of these tastes, which is an opportunity to recognize a message coming from your body.

If you long for a taste of something sweet, you can be sure that your body is telling you it wants some quick energy because almost anything with a sweet taste is fueled by sugar or another simple carbohydrate that the body can translate into an energy rush. The tongue may remember its first taste this side of the womb -- the sweet concentrated colostrum of the mother's breast, or even the chemical sweetness of baby formula. This kind of association is quite likely to activate the Emotional Body that will equate the sweetness with emotional experiences. The tongue represents the organ of the heart in Chinese medicine and thus the tongue, with its attending taste buds, can often play the trickster. I often say to my children, "Don't eat for your tongue, eat for your body."

Back on the other side, within the womb, the first taste was indubitably that of the salty amniotic fluid. The "peeping Tom" faculty of ultrasound has caught tiny fetuses sucking their thumbs in the womb. Perhaps this explains why we are all so salt crazy. Even though it hardens the arteries, and creates all manner of imbalance, we insist on ingesting it in disastrous quantities. The blood in our veins is salty and very similar in composition to that of the sea. My own theory is that our primordial memories of our marine origin insatiably tugs at our very core, causing us to revisit our source by attempting to ingest its essence. Salt is a very yang energy and our thirst for it is a driving force. Once we start eating something salty, we will often continue, just for the taste of the salt, long after the desire for the food itself has subsided.

Both sour and bitter tastes represent a cry for help by the digestive system of the body. Each of these will cause the saliva and digestive fluids to flow rather profusely. They are both astringent and will jolt the digestive juices to perform their tasks. Some people say that the body is as young as its digestive system is strong. It is logical that the body must be able to digest and absorb nutrients in order to maintain optimal health. In many countries, bitter and sour substances are a part of daily, if not seasonal preventive routine for health. Perhaps because most things that are poisonous are bitter, the body will come alive when just a small amount of a bitter substance is ingested. Sour flavors also cause the body to come alert in vivid response. Just think of how the taste of a sour lemon felt in your mouth when you were a child.

Your body offers you great pleasure in the sense of taste connected to the quality of texture. Much of your food preference is based on the association of taste to texture. For example, consider the texture of an artichoke, the silkiness of a caracole, or the weight of whipped cream on your tongue.

Sensitivity to taste often diminishes with age; perhaps not so much because the sensory neurons are actually nonfunctional, as that you have stopped caring about the joy of eating. All the senses of the body need to be trained, refined and exercised in order to keep it acutely aware and excited about life! Your body needs your directive and participation in communing with you in these sensory ways.

THE SIXTH SENSE

The "sixth" sense is what has always been referred to as the psychic sense. The psychic quality of subtle communion is actually what this entire book is about. You can experience accurate and detailed knowing about your body by meditating on it and simply allowing it to express its state of being to you. You might call it psychic awareness because the communication is most like a knowing: you "feel" the information, rather like a telepathic conversation.

One of the most informative explorations within your body is the intuitive art of listening on symbolic levels to the stories the body wishes to tell you. Not only does the brain record every bump of the knee, but conversely it causes the knee to be bumped to alleviate pent up or negative energy that has become stuck there. The body is like a road map of the soul's lessons. Each part of the body is symbolic of a certain theme, and its very function expresses that theme. For example, the left side of the body corresponds to the feminine, yin or receiving energies. The hands direct energies in and out of the body. If you were to hurt your left hand or wrist, it would suggest that your body is trying to show you that you are stopping the flow of energy coming into you, or that you are afraid to utilize your own intuitive

skills. This is a dilemma often visited on men who may have a sensitive nature, but who are embarrassed to express it. The fear of being loved, with its attendant feelings of unworthiness, also plays in here. I find this kind of body language a fascinating and accurate translation of messages from the body. Of course, if one could listen to the body, it wouldn't have to go to such extremes. You can well imagine that there are hundreds of these relationships corresponding to different parts of the body; but they will have to wait for another book. Even better, just ask your own body to explain itself symbolically to you and you will be astounded at the information you receive. You can discover the messages by listening with your sixth sense.

When something negative happens in your body, whether it is a disease or an accident, it is very important to tune your consciousness into that part and let yourself perceive what your body is saying. If you are willing to explore the "purpose" of the experience, the body quite often will reward you by healing with miraculous speed since it no longer needs the manifestation of its thematic concern.

The seventy senses teach you to recognize in minute detail the workings of your body on multi-levels that include chemical, electromagnetic and telepathic. Through a myriad of exquisitely delicate perceptions of pressure, distance, spacial relationship, density and other fascinating senses, you can know what is happening inside you. Through these perceptions, you can experience the workings of your endocrine system and the humming vibrations of your atoms!

THE HUM OF YOUR ATOMS

One of the most powerful ways to commune with your body is to focus on the atomic level. It is said that Jesus the Christ performed all his healings by instantaneously rebalancing atoms in which the electrons had gone out of sync. This is certainly important to us in today's world when free radicals caused by environmental abnormalities, especially radiation, are constantly bombarding our bodies. Twice I have broken bones and been able to heal them by focusing my attention on the electrons of the cells in the damaged area. Like a miracle, my bones mended within two days and I was poignantly reminded of my body's true capacities!

Just perceiving the atoms of your being will put you in a space to command the quality of your body's functioning. Try this. Sit in meditation and attune your consciousness within the atom of the cell. Just imagine that you are inside a cell in your body and move into the atoms. Inside the atom, the electrons spin in their figure eight patterning, causing a whirring or humming sound. This is the "sound" of your life force! If you allow yourself to perceive it, you will be in the most balanced and perfect state possible. Science says the atoms never die. They exist in a timeless, universal sea of cosmic proportion; through them you become truly **Ageless.**

If you pay attention in these ways, no negative energies could ever cause enough disruption outside your awareness to become dis-eased. Foreign bodies, radiation, heavy metals and other toxic waste, tumors and deposits, all become detectable by the subtle perception of your senses. Thus your body stays free of the destructive elements that make it age and die, while your "higher senses" of play, humor, creativity and transcendence keep you lively and **Ageless.**

REMEMBERING

One of the wonderful ways to communicate with your body is to contemplate memories your body has of its accomplishments. Allowing the body to communicate those experiences, helps you to change your point of view about who you are physically. It triggers your body to respond to the memory as if it were happening now. Your body remembers things you have long since forgotten. Yet each and every experience you have ever had is indelibly locked within your brain. Your body has its own score of accomplishments and failures. For example, ask your body what it loved to do the most as a child. Perhaps you loved to run, to jump, to swim or to dance. If you meditate on that running or dancing, your body's energy will be stimulated so that it can do these things again. It has all that memory stored within the mind of the cell and can bring it forward so that you enjoy the rush of feeling like a kid again. This excites the life force within your body. Perhaps this is why old people enjoy watching kids play so much. It makes them feel good just to remember. But if you can feel that child's magnificent energy **inside** you, the effect will be ever so much more than emotional or mental. The body seeks a model of identity. Just as you attempt to look a certain way or act a certain way in order to identify yourself, your physical body identifies the images, programming or messages you send it as its model about how it is. This is an incredible level of consciousness on the part of the body,

and a great tool for you. The body needs positive programming and encouragement. It is a little bit of the "I think I can" theme such as the story of "The Little Train that Could." As long as the brain is sending clear messages to the body, the body will respond to those messages as if they were real! Thus, the "I think I can, I think I can" will actually create "I did." All you have to do is be willing to make the choice, resist anxiety, doubt, and self-deprecating thought forms and replace them with feelings of honoring and supporting your body.

MENTAL COMMUNICATION

One of the fabulous discoveries about our bodies is their willingness to follow our command. Science has proven beyond a shadow of a doubt that the mechanisms and functioning of the body, which we have always considered outside of conscious control, can, in fact, be controlled through the conscious mind. Demonstrations of slowing the heart rate, lowering blood pressure and dropping the temperature of the hands are all clear examples that our conscious will can dictate to the body and the body will follow. People everywhere are learning to improve their health by performing these feats with the help of bio-feedback and other simple techniques that train them to focus their will and give the body clear commands.

One of the most intense bodily miracles that happened to me was a time when I had two sons on a Lacrosse team and I helped out as a trainer. We were in Colorado for a very important Lacrosse tournament. As I was watching the warm up, a stray ball came out of nowhere and smashed into my left eye, knocking me backward. I heard a loud cracking sound as it hit the orbit of my eye and several people later told me that they had heard the sound as well. There was a stunned hush as the team and coach stared at me. I put my hand over my eye and in a loud commanding voice said, " my eye is perfect, no bruise!" I stood in silent contact with my eye for quite a few minutes. When I took my hand away there was nothing but a tiny pink spot where the ball had collided with the orbit. For the team I used acupuncture and very strong blood-moving herbs to protect the boys from bruises, but the tincture could not be applied around the eyes so I placed two needles in the area and left them in during the game. There never appeared any swelling or bruising and the event was spoken of as if a miracle had taken place by everyone who witnessed it. This was not a case of convincing myself or my body, it was an absolute necessity. I could not be "off the team" as it were, and my body understood that. Parents often block illness from the body because they know that they must take care of their families and thus there is no allowance for such a time out as sickness.

If you can apply the recognition of this mental power over the body, there is no end to the creative and healthy applications you can employ. All of these conscious directions can and will be followed by the body through the powerful mandate of the mind that conceptualizes the structure of health. Thus you can understand how easy it is to command your endocrine system to release hormones in perfect harmony and balance, to stimulate the circulatory and fluid systems so that the nutrition available to the cells is without disruption and any debris is carried away. Whatever you are aware of that needs to be done in the body can be greatly facilitated by your mental command.

People around the world wake up at a certain hour each morning; not by the sun, but because they have mentally instructed their body to do so as they went to bed the night before. This "mind control" of the body was made famous by Jose Silva and is taught in almost every country in the world. He uses a simple method of counting to five and repetition of the command to imprint the message in the brain. It's application is almost unlimited. I use this technique when I am traveling and have no time to indulge my body in "jet lag." I tell it that it will be awake and alert and function on the same schedule as everyone else in the new time zone; unfailingly, it does.

At first it may seem strange that your body is listening to you as if it were another person, though, of course, it has mind in each of its trillions of cells that are ready to follow your direction. Can you imagine what this means? Someone is listening to your every thought!

If you make statements such as, "I'm too tired," or "I'm too old!" your body will believe you and become what you say it is. Think what you are doing when you habitually use cliches such as, "This old body, I'm getting old", or "this is a pain in the neck." I have often noted the correlation between someone who uses this expression and who also very obviously has little range of motion in the neck. The neck expresses the personal will where judgement and stubbornness reside.

Tell your body how wonderful it looks and how perfectly it functions and it will reward you by manifesting your prophecy. If you want to seriously work on your body, I suggest that you make an audio tape of all the things you want to program into your body's repertoire and listen to it in the car and especially as a last point in your bedtime routine. I will give you some examples that you might want to put on your tape. It is important to visualize your messages and enjoy the feelings they bring to you as you focus on them. Don't hurry through the list. State each command and feel it as if it were true at this moment, then slowly go on to the next.

*My body is **Ageless**. It is flexible and graceful and full of endless energy.*
My eyes are bright and clear and communicate wisdom. I can see perfectly. I see both the visible and invisible worlds.
My skin is clear and vibrant. I always smell good.
My hair is shiny and full.
My teeth and gums are healthy.
My muscles allow me to do anything I want. I am strong.
My heart pumps effortlessly and happily.
My heart loves to push my blood throughout my body to nourish me.
My lungs are feeding me oxygen and pure prana.
My liver balances my energy needs and detoxifies all poisons from my body.

My intestinal tract brings me perfect nourishment and eliminates what I don't need.

My urinary system filters and removes all unwanted substances from the fluids of my body.

My kidneys bring the deepest chi energy to feed my heart.

My nervous system is calm and efficient, relaying all information throughout the body.

My brain stores and accesses all memories and is always clear-thinking and creative.

*My endocrine system is in perfect balance. The gonads, pancreas, adrenals, thymus, thyroid, pituitary, hypothalamus and pineal glands all secrete the hormones I need in exactly the right amount and at the right time to support my **Ageless Body**.*

My immune system functions perfectly, never allowing disease producing agents or negative energies to gain hold in my body.

My auric field is strong and vibrant.

My Emotional Body is balanced and in contact with my spiritual essence through my Higher Self.

My face and being are radiant in health and happiness.

*I am an **Ageless** being with infinite grace and peace.*

*I have a truly **Ageless Body, Ageless Body, Ageless Body!***

You may want to add specific messages about parts of your body that need work. Perhaps hearing, knees or other aspects that need improvement will benefit from your mental and energetic programming. Remember to create an image or feeling that goes with each statement so that your command to the body carries a physical impact through this energetic conduit.

You are in for some wonderful surprises as you start communicating with your body on these new levels. It is incredible to acknowledge the companionship of the cloak you wear throughout your life. Yours is a "talking body," willing to give you reams of fascinating data about yourself, not only at this very moment, but its entire history of recorded imprints throughout this lifetime and beyond.

AGELESS EMOTIONS

*"The **Ageless Body** bears a quality of emotions that are light and joyous, willing to experience ecstasy and the richness of life at any moment."*

Every human heart is born with the memory of absolute rapture and magnificent fullness that come from being part of the universal energies. At the moment of conception, the limitless bliss of the cosmos squeezes down into the finite structure of human form and experiences the fear of separation. At this pivotal point, the Emotional Body emerges from its storehouse of memory and inhabits its space on the matrix of the genetic fabric.

It is under the direction of the Emotional Body that your life unfolds; unfolds into strife, stress and negativity, or into a kind of expansive, unlimited playful self that provides the pure energy of an **Ageless Body**. Only unconditional love, with its unceasing stream of compassion and encouragement, will produce **ageless** living. You can teach yourself to reinterpret your life and all the experiences you have so that you feel emotionally clear and willing to perceive the joyful aspects of living. To do this you must explore your Emotional Body at great depth so that you can surrender the old negative conclusions that constrain you from the higher realms of ecstatic existence. Wherever the victim remains in your emotional psyche, there is the limit of your emotional repertoire. If you still see yourself in the clutches of some external force, then you cannot truly comprehend the choices you have made on a soul level. The **Ageless Body** is activated by the cellular mind of the physical body that has recorded the echos of laughter issuing forth from an Emotional Body that is capable of feeling the true self, the Higher Self, and thus realizes the game of life.

Because the mind is so powerful, the thought-forms that govern the Emotional Body's conclusions about who you are actually influence the life force energy available to you. If you have thought-forms that belittle your physical body, your body will follow suit and become what you most fear, resist or despise.

If you experience disappointment in relationship, you will tend to focus your self-rejection through your body, as if to blame it for not being worthy enough to catch the love you desire. Negative thoughts you have such as, "nobody would want this old body, I hate my thighs, hair, chest, " send messages to the body that are tallied up and eventually produce consequences. The physical body will close itself down in the same way the Emotional Body shuts down from life. It imprints this negativity and translates it into blockages of energy, until ultimately the cells are choking in the pollutions of thought turned into poison.

Thus the body ages because it tires of the endless verbal, mental and physical abuses thrust upon it by the violent and unquenchable Emotional Body. The Emotional Body uses the physical body as a ploy to get the love it needs to survive. It demands the touch, the hug and the sexual encounter to assure itself that it exists. Forcing the physical body to carry the brunt of emotional tyranny is a grave injustice, for it is only one avenue of perception. You can teach your Emotional Body to identify love and experience pleasure in other ways as well!

THE MEASURE OF LOVE

Feelings of lack of love are main contributors to the aging process. In most relationships, we are acutely aware of the balance of emotional energy between ourselves and the other. We continually measure the power we feel by who expresses or extends the most emotion. This causes an overshadowing of anxiety because overt expression almost never equates actual feeling. Men, for example, rarely are able to show their deepest feelings of love in the same manner as women. Perhaps this is why women waste so much energy worrying about whether men love them or not. Meanwhile, men bear their feelings deeply hidden, so that they are prisoners of powerful forces that could otherwise amplify their enjoyment of life.

Most people measure love by the symbolic gestures they have learned from their own family. How the mother and father expressed affection towards each other and their children becomes the yardstick for future expression. This creates a great deal of confusion between partners because one may be waiting for words, while the other is looking for loving acts. We measure love in terms of our own repertoire and therefore miss infinite variations of loving gestures intended for us because we do not recognize the form of its expression.

When our measuring reveals that we receive the lesser amount of love, we may create a weapon of emotional vindictiveness against ourselves, as often the measure of another's love becomes the measure of our own. This is a great tragedy because the capacity to give love has almost nothing to do with the person who receives it. It has everything to do with the fear of loving and the degree of safety one feels. However, most of us imagine that a scarcity of love is because we lack beauty, intelligence or money, rather than because the one we love is ultimately afraid to risk the giving.

If a relationship ends, we turn the loss of love into self-reprisal, heaping fury or depression on ourselves because someone else does not choose us. All negative thoughts towards ourselves set up energies that encircle us and affect the body's will to live. Even young people can become physically ill and terminally lethargic if they punish themselves over the powerlessness to control another's choice. When another person says no to relationship, we have the choice either to mourn the loss, or to embrace the freedom.

CONCLUSION: THE LIMITATION OF CHOICE

One of the most dangerous attributes of the Emotional Body is its habit of drawing conclusions so that it can respond or react to its experiences within some kind of foundation of safety. Fixating on a conclusion is a defense mechanism of the Emotional Body that plays havoc with any true assessment of our worth. It does this through the thought patterns of association. For example, "He didn't stay after making love so he really doesn't love me." The conclusion is that the time given is equal to quantity of love. This association may well be coming from childhood feelings that daddy didn't spend enough time and therefore really didn't love the child. Because the Emotional Body tends to repeat its experiences, this person will most likely always draw lovers who cannot stay until she becomes conscious of the pattern. The Emotional Body will feel justified in its conclusions of lack of love because they continue to reoccur without the realization that she is creating a reality based on an experience that did not access the input of the father. She will then conclude that she is not worthy of love and that somehow it is her lack or fault. The best way to break this vicious cycle of negative or faulty conclusions is to teach the Emotional Body to focus on the gift of each experience, rather than the fear of denial. Instead of giving all the power of choice to the other person, the focus could be on one's own intention to express love, which is independent of the other's reactions and thus much more fulfilling.

NEGATIVITY, THE TIME BOMB OF AGING

Negative thoughts and feelings weaken the body physically. The immune system is all but completely interrupted by severe emotional stress. This is the reason people often succumb to colds when they are holding negative feelings. Stress that comes from chronic anxiety drains the adrenals and precipitates attack by foreign organisms which have been lurking around waiting for a weak link in the system. When the body cannot prevent invasion, it begins to tire of the fight. You know how difficult it is to maintain an optimistic outlook when you feel poorly. It is as if the body can no longer remember health or power or happiness.

Negative thoughts and depressive feelings are like a time bomb of aging because the body simply begins to manifest its helplessness and lack of purpose by withering away. Aging is the result. The body will close down just like the Emotional Body does. Without a strong will to meet life, it no longer performs its duties of self-protection and cellular rejuvenation.

Negativity not only reflects itself in the inner organs, but the energies we feel express themselves on the outside of our bodies as well. It is not difficult to know how someone feels about life as you look at their face. The eternally furrowed brow, the mouth that tilts downward, the crease between the eyebrows, all speak of the anger and sorrows entrapped in the flesh. The face is a very important reservoir of emotions. Anger is stored in the TMJ joints that articulate the jaws, as well as in the eyes. When someone doesn't like something or someone, they instinctively narrow their eyes. The eyes reflect the liver, which is a natural storage place for anger as it controls the energy in the body.

Within the cheeks are the storage places of tears and people with round, full faces are known for their deep emotions.

Very often the muscle of the diaphragm itself is so laden with emotional residue that even the pure breath does not circulate through the trunk of the body. We also hide feelings under the armpits and along the sides of the ribs. Most of us become ticklish in these areas fairly early in life. This comes from the solar plexus area around the stomach which is the interface of the Emotional Body with the physiological body. The entire abdominal region is a depository for emotions. Many years ago I noticed that if you touch some one's abdomen, they very quickly begin to express their emotions. Psychics and sensitive people, including men, often develop rotund stomachs in an attempt to protect themselves from their emotional vulnerability, as if the flesh could somehow hide them from the emotional energies of others, as well as their own.

SABOTAGING THE POSITIVE

All too often, the moment that we feel ecstasy or bliss, the Emotional Body will respond with an "afterthought" that warns, "But this won't last! Tomorrow will be just the same." It is a kind of perverse way to protect itself from the disappointment it expects to follow any good feelings. Afterthoughts can and must be controlled if you hope to train your body to hold a positive course of continual transcendence and **ageless** health. Whenever you discover your Emotional Body whispering disparaging thoughts, immediately erase them by replacing them with positive imagery and energy. When the afterthought tries to bring ecstasy back down to the sensation of numbness, give it a faster energy to dissolve it. At The Light Institute, we use the technique of sending it a color, releasing it through the force of motion, out of the body. You can spin it out, dance, sing or hum it out, so that your awareness goes back to the supportive and positive feelings of the self.

There is a natural rhythm in the universe, which is expansion/contraction. However, the contraction does not need to be contraction into fear or conclusion, but rather contraction into manifestation, whereby you use higher energies to help you accomplish your goal. You can feel the ecstasy and then translate its energy into your daily life so that whatever you are doing is filled with pleasure. Perhaps you feel numb because you think you are unimportant, that the job you do is irrelevant. But, if you can bring feelings of ecstasy into the job you do, your very presence becomes an incredible gift that will alter the lives of everyone around you. It is not the job itself but the peace and encouragement you bring to the environment around you that is of untold value to everyone.

RELEASING NEGATIVITY

You are not stuck with negative thought-forms or feelings. You can consciously choose to replace them by practicing powerful and pleasurable techniques to awaken your awareness of your **Ageless Body.**

WATER, THE EMOTIONAL HEALER

Water is a wonderful vehicle to clear or transmute emotional energies. Not only does it soothe the body, but it comforts the spirit. Whenever you find yourself feeling caught by your emotions, find a body of water to wash your aura and reset your electromagnetic field. Whether it is a bath, shower, lake or sea, even a splash over the face and head, water will help you to clear away emotional debris so that you can change your negative imprints.

Water has always been the symbol of emotion. Visions and dreams that include images of the sea and other bodies of water are said to describe the state of the Emotional Body. If one perceives a stormy sea or muddy water, it is an expression of the turbulent feelings that are pushing to be released. It is common for people to dream of sewage or toilets that graphically express the "unspeakable" energies pent up inside of the Emotional Body.

The highest, most elevated faculties of the human psyche such as intuition, psychic awareness and clairvoyance are also an intrinsic part of the emotional make-up as we bring it into contact with the spiritual body. Here lie the crystal clear lakes, and vast translucent seas in which we can mirror our very soul.

BREATH

One of the greatest ways to move through negativity is to use the breath. The breath moves the consciousness on all levels. If you begin to breathe deeply and slowly, you will find it difficult to hold onto anger. Breathing reminds you to receive. If you feel neglected or unloved, try laying down and breathing deeply for at least five minutes. Mark the time and gulp in the breath, or just breathe as if each breath is a gift someone has given you and you are swallowing it with pleasure. Air can give you a sensation of fullness that the Emotional Body will experience as satisfaction. If you consciously receive breath, you are telling your body that you are willing to live.

MUSIC, THE CONDUCTOR OF HIGHER EMOTIONS

Sound is one of the most powerful energies available to alter the emotional octave. Both our physical, as well as our subtle bodies, resonate to sound vibrations that can make a great difference in mood and feeling. People are becoming more aware of this opportunity to be uplifted by sound. The great composers always used this emotional connection to sound to enhance a more powerful response to their music. Opera is a classic example of the emotional charge that can be activated by the dramatic use of the human voice as well as forceful instrumentation.

At the Nizhoni School for Global Consciousness, our students enjoy the art of drumming. Drumming allows them to express their own rhythms that create a synchro-nous pulse with the beat of their bodies. The heart beat, organ pulses and cerebral spinal pulse all contribute to a delicate sense of centering that helps the Emotional Body find peace.

People today are beginning to use the sounds of nature to relax and open themselves to higher conscious levels. Nature reminds us of our place in the universe which has a very healing effect on our psyche. It is important to explore sounds that take you up through the heart into the vast realms of heightened awareness so that your sense of yourself becomes a perception of connectedness to all of life.

THE INNER CHILD

Transmuting negativity comes easily if you take your attention off the outer world and seek deeply within yourself. Of the essence energies that come from the center of your being, one of the most powerful is your Inner Child. Not only were you once a child that perceived reality differently than you do today, but that child was a bridge to your universal soul. The Inner Child holds great wisdom and the kind of joyful energy that can immediately lift you from despair into ecstasy.

There is an incredible power and tenderness belonging to the child. It comes from the capacity to continually let go and allow whatever is in focus to carry the child into a new adventure. In fact, it takes very little effort for our lives to be an adventure. Adults make this difficult because they place so many constrictions on the outcome, whereas the child simply plays for the adventure itself. The more simple you are willing to be, the more ecstatic and blissful energies can be absorbed into your being. The best pathway is the intention to absorb all the beauty that is there; to use life.

In order to create or experience **ageless** emotions, you must be willing to continually embrace your Inner Child. It is the aspect of your Emotional Body most able to forgive, risk and experience ecstatic states. The Inner Child always activates an incredible exuberance of energy that can help you feel young and alive. Most adults have completely lost touch with their Inner Child and have forgotten the sense of an eternal "now." Ask yourself now, what is enough for you at this moment. It is this quality of what you can experience and call forth to yourself at any moment, that bridges the gap to the future or the past.

The secret of **ageless** emotions is to live in the present and choose healing and divine feelings rather than negative ones. Once you realize that you have a choice, you are set free. You can help yourself silence the chattering mind, the doubtful negativity of the rational being, by allowing all of your subtle bodies to come to the stillpoint of your knowing; it is your Spiritual Body that sets you free. Once having said, "I choose laughter!" you have in your command unlimited possibilities in terms of how you bring that laughter to you; whether it is a book, a movie, a friend or a place that delights you, your Inner Child can deliciously select the scenario.

The child is ready for growth because his reality is in his "being" and he therefore feels perfectly safe. It is the parent who worries, because the adult is caught in the "doing," which is a step removed from his center and he is no longer in touch with the safety of being. Your Inner Child will say, "I am good enough, therefore I am safe. If I make a mistake, I learn, but the learning will not kill me, I'll still be there at the end of the learning." The Emotional Body develops the illusion of drawing conclusions in order to be safe. A very good exercise is to find your point of safety. Ask yourself, "Where is the point of safety in me? Am I safe in my genitals, my mind, or in my heart?" You will learn a lot about how you have structured your reality and relationships by doing this. When you can give your body the message, "I am safe," you will be free to become **ageless.**

One of the interesting dilemmas between the child and the adult is the issue of "What is the consequence of my action?" Children must learn to contemplate the consequence of their action, but they must learn it as a part of the capacity to choose, not from the place of judgement and fear. In other words, the conclusion doesn't have to be that which is dangerous. The adult thinks, "If I take this choice, will it be dangerous for me?" The child thinks, "If I take this choice, where will it take me?"

For the powerful Inner Child, any exploration is enough to bring about bliss because there is the cosmic awareness that everything is a part of a larger whole within an ever-expanding hologram. The Inner Child will teach you that each endeavor takes you on to the next one. You are a divine spark, therefore you are enough. You do not have to change that divine spark, you only need to BE it, to emanate and radiate it. You already contain all the wisdom you seek because you are alive, and that is the greatest knowing in the universe. All of your subtle bodies know exactly how to manifest health and vitality, but you must teach yourself to listen to them.

VELOCITY AND AGELESS EMOTIONS

Just as the energy of the child is faster than that of the adult, the **ageless** emotions are attuned to a kind of velocity that assists you in quickening your energetic frequency to embrace such feelings as ecstasy, bliss and rapture. Emotion contains motion, and thus the explanation of feeling light or as if flying, describes the sensations of the upper octave of emotional range. The very velocity of the higher emotions changes who you are, helping you to be a full and loving being who does not need to hold on. Some people are as afraid of ecstatic feelings as they are of depression because there is not the comfortable holding pattern of control that commonly stifles any emotional expansion. When you can free yourself from fear of the motion, you can truly be childlike and **ageless.**

It is important to give your Emotional Body the experience of velocity. At the Light Institute we teach people the power of spinning so that the cells of the body actually feel the sensation of motion and letting go. Detachment is not about losing the experience of the thing you desire, but rather about allowing it to wash through you while the velocity moves you onward. The velocity expands your consciousness so that you begin to see more of the hologram. You see more that can please and delight you, and at that speed you can perceive the synchronicity which helps you to let go. The moment you see the purpose of any relationship or experience, you no longer have the need to cling. The clinging comes because you are afraid there will be nothing after that and you will lose the self; whereas the faster you spin, the more the self extends out, so that you experience that not only are you always there, but that everything is in you!

FEELING

Ageless emotion utilizes the incredible capacity of the human vehicle to experience feeling, not only feeling in terms of joy or ecstasy, but in the actual contact that brings comfort by its inherent recognition. For example, if you can feel the texture or pattern of a flower, your body will merge with it. The more you seek to experience nature and your connection to all that is, the less you will contract your feelings. You will discover that you can receive the most delicious love from non-human form and that this communion makes you whole. You are no longer alone!

To quicken the Emotional Body so that it can become **ageless**, you must consciously experience the pulsation of the universe which brings perpetual change; there is life and death, day and night. Feel yourself a part of the stars so that when you are in contraction, you recognize the choice to feel that you are part of the stars, nature or the love of children, so that your attention is turned away from the conclusion and reaches out to the universe. If the Emotional Body can experience continual velocity and motion, it becomes easier for it to let go.

If you can experience emotions as a sense of velocity and motion, then there is not the "stuckness" that entraps you or makes you feel heavy. Let life bring its gifts to you, even if they cause you to grow by letting go. As each gift comes, you become fuller and lighter and therefore can embrace more. The more fulfilled you are, the more you are able to give, so that the giving becomes the incredible game of life.

THE POWER OF THE GIVER

In order to truly embrace **ageless** emotions, you must be willing to detach yourself from the dependency of emotional exchanges from others. This is a new exercise for the very small human being who has no repertoire of detachment and, at the same time, fullness. The detachment from need will free you so that you can access an unlimited stream of those high emotions that perhaps you only experienced in your childhood: unconditional love, complete delight in the self, exuberance of feeling that the heart can soar -- not because the outside world fulfills your dream, but because within the energies of soaring are all the elements necessary to merge with the cosmos, the source of all energy.

The choice to say, "I am full, I have enough to give to you," is the secret of **ageless**ness. **Ageless**ness depends on the capacity to be the giver, to be the channel of energy that moves through endless cycles of motion. If you can learn to master pure universal energy, you will never need to grow old. Whenever you feel empty and depleted, you are not accessing your energy source and that is what initiates aging. Immobilization stops the consciousness of the body from having enough energy, to get out of the lethargy and move from inertia back into being the source of life.

There is a sensation of extending in order to experience the freedom of **ageless** emotion. You have the right to reach out and draw energy to you that makes you feel complete. Do not surrender to the illusion that only other humans can nourish you. Take the limitless energy from the sun, the moon, earth, plants, animals and myriad other living forms whose radiant life can feed you.

A wonderful way to practice **ageless** emotion is to imagine yourself as a Great Being, experiencing that you are the source, not only of everything you desire, but also the force of distribution and dissemination of all that you love. Think about the kinds of experiences and energies you would give away. If you hunger for laughter, imagine that you are the one that brings laughter to those around you. As you become the conduit for the higher emotions, you can experience how you yourself are renewed and altered by the presence of that energy, which you, with all your creative force, design.

USING LIFE

Life is the gift of your soul. Embodiment allows you to see the laws of the universe in action. You can learn how to manifest and transmute energies so that all you create is magnificent. Life is for you to use; life is not here to devour you. The question is always like the child's, " What shall I do with this?" And as long as you are willing to receive the gift, then you are using life and you can never be entrapped by it, as you are the one that is the source. You are here to spend life and the more you spend it, the more there is -- the more **ageless** it becomes, and it is always renewable!

SEXUALITY, THE EMOTIONAL TRIGGER

Sexuality is a great test for the Emotional Body because it triggers all of the deep feelings we carry about ourselves. Until puberty the sexual connection to our sense of self is vague because it is not a part of how we address the world outside us. Once past puberty, the biological pull of procreation brings into play the presentation of the body as the major lure to gain a mate, and thus to procreate. This is painful for most of us as we begin to measure our self-worth on a scale of physical attributes. The temptation to wield our body as a lure becomes very great and at the same time, as we compare ourselves with other competitors, we begin to feel insecure about our value. Up until this point in life, we might have attained a goal through sheer drive or effort; but now there seems to be nothing outside of some mystical attraction mechanism, that does not yield to trying, or to any other discipline we might have learned, to bring us what or who we want.

The process of sexual maturation is an incredible vortex of energy that sucks us in and then thrusts us out into a frightening and competitive world where we tend to use our sexuality as a sword of emotional defense, even after we have found our partners and should be settling down to a "comfortable" life. As long as we view ourselves in the marketplace of desirability in terms of the physical body, we will remain in a prison of anxiety and insecurity. Perhaps this is why we tend to use sexual energy as an emotional weapon, rather than the divine gift of loving that it truly is.

We will always desire to touch and be touched by another as long as the veil of separation from our true source remains a part of human experience. Indeed, the sensuality of the body is one of the many gifts given to us to support and encourage the enjoyment of embodiment. However, the blissful feelings of closeness are there to enhance profound communion, rather than as a cloak to hide in.

In love relations, it is difficult to separate the closeness we seek from the dependency it instills in us *vis a vis* our partners. We project onto them the power to make us happy and then feel utterly helpless to find a sense of fulfillment without them. We are especially dependent on them for sexual pleasure. This is a very inflammable situation because the performance of lovemaking becomes so identified with the message of being loved, or not.

Many of the fights between two people stem from harboring feelings about what happens or does not happen during sexual expression. You can free yourself from this web of emotion by realizing that **you** are entirely responsible for the sensations that you have in your body. Begin by asking yourself if you are willing to be present in your body, and then ask your body if it can feel your presence! The gift of sensuality can be focused in any direction; for example, caressing a rose could be totally orgasmic if you are willing to allow that degree of involvement. If you seek spectacular sexual fulfillment, you must come to know your own body in intimate detail so that when your partner touches you, you can **use** that touch to carry the stimulation as far as it can go, - which depends completely on your capacity to focus on the sensation and amplify it.

You may have not yet discovered your own sensuality and are still hoping someone will show it to you. You do not recognize your own timeless bodies and **ageless** emotions, because you have forgotten who you are. Your connection to the spark of life comes from inside you and it is **ageless**. It is not dependent on your emotional ties with the outside world, but rather on your relationship with your own body.

You can learn to experience sexual energy as pure energy in and of itself, which will lead you to what I called "Cosmic Orgasm" as I described it in my book, *Ecstasy is a New Frequency*. These are the higher realms of sexual experience that happen throughout the entire body, rather than just the genitals, as it aligns to new frequencies. People are beginning to experience these rare octaves of sexuality and this will set in motion a new kind of sexuality that is not based on what you can extract from a partner, but rather the intensity of energy available to you, with or without a partner!

If you can learn to move deeply within your body, you can use it as a finely tuned instrument of loving expression that you share with your partner, rather than passively waiting for the other to bring the energy to you.

Sexual energy is instrumental to the **Ageless Body**. It is through the hormones connected to sexual function, nudging us towards procreation, that the body stays in a perpetual state of "juicy" youth. However, that heightened activity of the sexual- physical body can be transformed into a higher octave energy that nourishes the entire multidimensional Being. It can be brought up from its base in the genitals and fed through the endocrine glands to create an infinite helix of **ageless** energy.

If you are in the menopausal era of your life, or a man past the age of thirty-five years, then it is crucial for you to access your sexual energy not only on genital levels, but to also preserve and awaken it to serve your whole body. If you do the endocrine exercises and the exercises for Eternity, you will be able to keep your physical body young, radiant and full of life. Since sexual energy is the creative force of the universe, you can extend it to rejuvenate yourself and heal others, as well as open creative channels you never dreamed existed. Your conscious intention can lead you from the valley of despair into the ecstatic heights that are your true nature.

AGELESS CONSCIOUSNESS

Ageless consciousness is a timeless state of mind which includes and utilizes the body for its expression. The body is innately a fluid form in motion capable of profound and living peace. When the body reaches a state of liquid grace, there is a coursing of energy that pulses out from its very core, caressing the inner organs and bursting out into the auric field. This is a natural state for the body. If you let your body guide you and you simply move in any direction it pulls you, there will be a cessation of mind chatter. Since there is nothing outside the reach of an intuitive and creative mind, all things and feats are possible. In these eternal moments the mind and the body join and you are gifted the blissful energy that has been lost within you.

When you can rest awhile in the present and encourage yourself that it is enough for you, there comes a kind of peace that floods through the body and the mind ceases to scold and limit. Consciousness brings the mind into higher octaves of awareness that free the Emotional Body. As it is freed from the prison of its doubt and separation, it effortlessly floats up to the lighted realms where ecstasy and bliss reside. The **Ageless Body** bears a quality of emotions that are light and joyous, willing to experience ecstasy and the richness of life at any moment.

WATER: THE SOURCE OF IT ALL

"The fluidity of water can teach us that we are not solid, immobile beings, but rather, ever changing yet powerful channels of life."

One of the most important keys to the **Ageless Body** is the recognition of how water affects your life. You probably never think about water as an element that is crucial to your vitality and health, and yet you can become dangerously dehydrated within a very short time if you do not drink water. It is through the liquid systems of the body that all nutrients are carried to the cellular level and the toxins are transferred away and out of the body. Living systems can carry on almost indefinitely only if they are not poisoned by their own wastes and can continually be flooded by essential nutrients.

Based on this fact, I have several times suggested to relief organizations that water, saturated with vitamins and amino acids, be delivered to people in starvation situations. One of the tragedies is that small children who survive famine suffer irreversible brain damage because of the lack of nutrients. If nursing mothers could be given such potentialised water, many lives would be saved.

Water not only feeds you and carries out the trash, it awakens your psyche, soothes your emotions and acts as the transmitter for all manner of information about you and your world. The first cell of your existence is nourished by it, and the enzymes and hormones that guard your life float in this magnificent medium. Water is truly the source of it all!

WATER: THE SACRED FLOW

Water is one of the sacred elements of our planet. Within our solar system only Earth and Mars (with its "dead" seas) contain this precious source from whose sacred flow comes the river of all life. Everything living here began in the tepid seas that once covered our planet which is even today, two-thirds water. Our primordial liquid origin is echoed within the very essence of our genetic pattern. The womb in which we grow is filled with saline amniotic fluid. Here we thrive for nine months, floating in our own sea, not very differently than we did millions of years ago. The blood carried in our veins is structured almost identically to sea water. The sea is our mother, our womb, and is therefore sacred to us all.

We must regain our sense of oneness with this element of our genesis so that we can remember our place in the vast universe.

Any substance that is necessary to life carries a sacred energy by virtue of its connection to Source. It is an intimate, symbiotic friend to us, calling upon our awareness to engage with it, uphold it and protect its quality so that we remain healthy and filled with its life-giving essence. Water is a sacred flow that moves within all layers and parts of our being as well as around and through our external environment.

Every religion uses water as a part of its expression of Divinity and Holiness. "Holy water" bestows the touch of protection and purification to the millions of Catholics as they enter and leave the sanction of their church. Babies are christened and baptized by the touch of water to signify rebirth into the spiritual life. Healing ceremonies often take place at the chosen lap of sacred waters. To lakes and springs, rivers and oceans, humanity brings its ills and sorrows to be healed.

Almost everyone enjoys submerging themselves in water and feels the comfort it provides. A long warm bath is one of the best antidotes for feelings of emptiness or loneliness. Within the deep recesses of our being, each of us longs to return to our source to be comforted in that almost forgotten essence of unconditional love, without which life often seems so difficult that we can hardly hold onto this world we must survive in. Our bodies never seem to outdistance the comfort of the waters in the womb.

I'll never forget the inconsolable crying my newborn son, Bapu, experienced when he was wrenched from the watery sea of his birthplace in the Bahamas, and brought to the high dry desert of New Mexico. He cried in abject agony for hours and hours until finally it occurred to me to try a warm bath. Almost the instant he heard the sound of water, he heaved a huge sigh and feel asleep. I lifted him tenderly into the bath and we both slept for several hours. After that, we spent part of each day in the water where he thrived and moved with the freedom and command of a natural water being.

These memories of our source let us experience a kind of relaxation in the bath that we do not feel in our environment of air. Perhaps for this reason the ancients in all parts of the world used water as a vital healing remedy. Water provides a weightless environment and helps healing by taking the pressure off inner organs. It is a wonderful help for the discomforts of stomach-ache and intestinal cramping. When we soak in the bath, the age-producing worries and frustrations seem to drain away.

YOU ARE WATER!

Water is the conduit for all the nutrients, hormones, enzymes and other vital elements that determine your health. Your blood, which is the transport for most of these substances, is 92% water. You could survive for days or even weeks without food, but without water, you would last only several days before dehydration brought death.

When you were born, you were about 97% water! By the time you are an adult, you have begun to dry up and are now only about 70% water. This is especially significant as it signals an alteration in the basic composition that reflects the hardening, stiffening and even dying in the body as it ages. Some say that aging is very much a process of dehydration. So many of the features of old people reflect this quality of dryness -- the wrinkled face and hands, leathered skin and most importantly, the drying up of the hormones that supply the vitality or "juice" to our lives.

Even that 70% of water in your body is astounding if you stop to think of yourself as a fluid being. To contemplate that you are more than half water will make you feel yourself differently. It means that the properties and the quality of water in your body have a far-reaching effect on who you actually are!

DETOXIFICATION

One of the most crucial functions of water is its capacity to clear away wastes and detoxify the body. If it were not for this help, the body would soon die in its own toxic soup. If you become toxic, there is no way for nourishment and life enhancing energy to break through to the cellular level. Not only is there the debris from unabsorbed food in your body, but there is also the almost insurmountable amount of inert fillers and other trash that must be separated from the food substances you ingest.

Huge quantities of chemical pollutants are mixed with the food you eat in an effort to make artificial foods more palatable and to preserve dead or denatured produce. Imagine the quantity of chemicals coming from the environments in which the food is grown, as well. Insecticides, herbicides and inorganic fertilizers have provided food for the masses, but are now subsequently causing chaotic and cancerous growths in ourselves and our children. We seem to be struggling to understand that nature cannot be tampered with, without disastrous side-effects coming into play as the result of short term need.

This short term approach on living bodies has never been a safe solution to our problems because the future arises from the present and any damage done to the body out of immediate need has ongoing effects in the not so distant future. People whose bodies have become addicted to alcohol, sugar and drugs all clutch at the hopeful illusion that an immediate need eclipses the probable outcome of destruction to the body, even though it tries to forewarn of the present danger. The body fights to rid itself of such damaging substances by releasing the flow of enzymes, hormones and other substances into the liquid medium that will facilitate the organs of elimination to remove them. Pollutants in the air, water and soil fill up our lungs, stick in our joints, and bombard our organs until the body can hardly stay afloat in the deluge.

Even more intrinsic to our toxic conditions are the emotional residues that plague our conscious and unconscious states. Fear and anger drastically affect our nervous system by dumping chemical reactions into the bloodstream that alter the brain's chemistry and actually lay down their negative imprint in the cells of the joints, organs and muscular system of the body. The synovial fluid in our joints causes swelling when it retains emotions or is sent messages by the Emotional Body to hold on. This is often the case in arthritis when the crystallization of minerals and negativity occur around the joints prohibiting the free flow of energy. The synovial fluid often increases in an attempt to ease the "friction" that is the result of the holding.

If the interstitial fluids are clear and the liquid systems of the body -- the lymph, blood and cerebro-spinal -- are clean, they can bring the nutrients to the cells and the cells can absorb those liquids and throw off toxins.

Fortunately, the fluid medium of our bodies can dilute, transport and neutralize toxins. Like the ever present tide, water washes through all our joints, organs, cells, interstitial spaces, circulatory, lymphatic and spinal systems to nourish, restore and detoxify.

PROPERTIES OF H₂O

From this short description of toxicity, you can see how important it is to drink, drink and drink more water to keep your body clean, functioning and **ageless**. The old medical adage has always been to drink at least eight glasses of water a day.

For some of us, imbibing so much liquid may be next to impossible. Drinking anything has always been hard for me. It seemed to do with the swallowing. Perhaps this is influenced by the fact that I had both whooping cough and diphtheria as a child, which may have left some subtle imprint about breathing and swallowing. I have met many others who have the same difficulty.

I discovered the answer in the research of Dr. Patrick Flanagan, one of the world's foremost scientists. Dr. Flanagan has spent many years seeking to duplicate the structure of the waters found in areas of the world where people tend to live significantly longer than "normal." These people live in clustered areas of high mountain regions such as the Hunza valley in India, Georgia of outer Mongolia, the Vilcabamba area of Ecuador and several mountain valleys in Peru and Bolivia.

Common to them all are glacier waters that feed their valleys. I remember drinking this "cloudy" and mysterious water on many of my treks throughout the mountainous regions of Bolivia. I saw it very symbolically as if the great mother glacier were overflowing her milk from her magnificent breasts to feed her children. I always felt very nourished by it. Glacier water is very similar to distilled water which is without mineral content. As the water flows down from the glacier it travels through mineral beds and absorbs special ionic minerals that charge it with life.

Dr. Flanagan's work describes a process by which water has a "wetting" quality that causes it to adhere to a substance with which it comes into contact and thereby wets it. The ability to do this depends on its electrical charge. The glacial water was highly charged by the colloidal mineral beds that imbued it with anionic (- ion) electrolytes.

Much of the water we drink has lost its charge because the organic colloids that provide the spark of life and the property of wetting, have been removed by the addition of chemicals and other cationic (+ ion) electrolytes to "treat" the water. This water always felt heavy to my throat and thus I was uncomfortable drinking it. Dr. Flanagan has found the way to duplicate the colloidal rich waters of the Hunzas that generate the elements of life force. He has created a concentrate of crystal colloids that can be added to water to bring it to life. Water that is enhanced with crystal colloids is wetter and literally slips down my throat like silk.*

My favorite water in the world is the fabulous VALSER Water from Switzerland. It trickles down from the snow capped Swiss Alps, traveling inward through massive layers of Grisons slate that nature thrust upward to the sky, and which add precious minerals. It descends down through beds of dolomite that add to its electrical charge and reaches a depth of 1000 meters (3,300 ft.) into the mountains. It is a curious *deja vu* effect because the journey of the water takes approximately 25 years to reach its home in a water cave. This means that it was created before the advent of contamination by acid rain and radiation! As the cave fills, the pressure builds and causes the water to be sent back up towards the surface as a warm (30° C) artesian well. I love the idea that it gushes up, still warm from its womb and is lifted out from 1,000 meters to be offered, pure and totally unspoiled, to nurture our bodies. VALSER Water is then allowed to aerate and is gently filtered through marble gravel and sand filters to remove excess iron. That's it. No more manipulation by man, just Mother Nature at its best.

The first time I tasted VALSER Water was when I was staying at the home of Donald and Joanna Hess in Bern, Switzerland. I was not in the habit of drinking much water but I knew I was quite dehydrated from traveling, so I poured a glass from the bottle that had been set in my room, and prepared to take just a sip. To my surprise, it was so smooth and easy to swallow that I finished all of it. I immediately went downstairs to inquire where it came from, only to discover that the Hess family happen to be the producers of VALSER Water and that they were as interested in the sacredness and protection of the earth's water as was I. Here began one of my life's greatest friendships!

After that I began to carry Valser Water with me when I traveled. Even though it is heavier because it is bottled in glass, it is recyclable and no dust enters the water the way it does through the pvc of plastic bottles.

WATER AWARENESS

There are many kinds of water that you might drink. Choices range from tap water to fancy bottled water, well water, carbonated, distilled or even reverse osmosis. Let's discuss them a bit so you can become more aware of how they might affect your body. Because water is so important to your **ageless body**, you really need to communicate with your body to see what kind of water it prefers. Your body knows whether you should drink any of these waters at any given time.

TAP WATER

Most city, or tap water has been so altered in order to remove the sewage from which it is reconstituted, that it is not recommendable. For example, chlorine is used to purify water in many areas of the world. There is considerable evidence that the striking rise in myocardial infarction seen in cities is directly related to the introduction of chlorine in municipal systems. Dr. Joseph Price, a scientist, published a book in 1969 called *Coronaries/Cholesterol/Chlorine* in which he gives very convincing evidence as to the correla-

tion between chlorine and arteriosclerosis. **

The inclusion of cationic minerals such as aluminum, for the purpose of coagulating and removing organic pollutants, has the secondary effect of destroying precious colloids. Even worse, municipalities also add excessive cationic salts to keep the water from corroding city pipes while those drinking such tap water may experience aggregation or clumping of their blood because of that same aluminum! Even these extreme measures to make water potable is no guarantee of its safety to drink. Some estimates purport that there are many thousands of carcinogens (cancer producing substances) in regular tap water.

BOTTLED WATER

All of this makes it very desirable to drink only special water. However, even bottled water suffers from the tampering by companies who first remove all the minerals and pollutants and then reconstitute the water. Unfortunately, except for a very few, the general understanding does not include awareness of the vital role of colloids in living systems and almost all water companies add cationic minerals whose formulas are not balanced in terms of energy-giving electrolytes, to reconstruct their water. Thus they destroy the precious life-giving colloids and give you mineral equations not appropriate for your delicate bodily system.

WELL WATER

Most well water is imbalanced by cationic minerals that necessitate some form of filtration. Because seepage from industrial run-off has begun to infiltrate deeper aquifers, spring or well water is risky business. Even more sobering is the question of what elements in the atmosphere water collects before it falls back to earth. Anything in the air can be absorbed into the water. We have already had a look at the damage caused by acid rain. We simply do not know the long range effects of contaminants such as those from jet aircraft, rockets, bomb tests and nuclear reactors. I have a suspicion that the steam from nuclear power plants is effecting the water vapor. All of these elements that become involved with water vapor have direct and potentially catastrophic results as they enter lakes, streams and rivers from which we draw our drinking water. Such "invisible" elements may be damaging our genetic material right now!

CARBONATED WATER

Carbonated water is a favorite around the world and yet the carbonation comes from the addition of carbon dioxide gas which is exactly what the body is attempting to rid itself of every time you exhale. CO_2 is a waste product within your body and is actually a poisonous gas carried by your blood to the lungs for expulsion. If you drink a lot of carbonated beverages, you will decrease your body's capacity to carry oxygen and put stress on your lungs which must get rid of the gas. Most of us have too much gas in our systems because of improperly combined foods that lead to indigestion and gas formation. We certainly do not need to add more!

DISTILLED WATER

Controversy rages on about the use or detriment of distilled water. Since it has no minerals, it tends to pull them from the body as it flushes the system. Thus it is a great cleanser, although it is also void of any life-giving quality. In truth, the great power of water is not the minerals it contains, but the electrical charge provided by its wonderful colloids that give it the gift of life-enhancing properties.

REVERSE OSMOSIS

Reverse osmosis is a method of removing dissolved solids and bacteria by forcing the water through a membrane. The water is then mineral free or neutral which helps to purify the body. At my house we drink reverse osmosis water that has the addition of a free-flow catalytic conditioner. The catalytic conditioner gives off natural colloids into the water by combining with metal alloys that create burmulian seed crystals. They are shed from the device into the water, forming negative ion particles. This gives me the best approximation of pure water with at least some of the attributes of anionic electrolytes. Dr. Flanagan's liquid crystal colloids are the state of the art, and perhaps one day all drinking water will be imbued with their life force qualities, just as Mother Nature intended.

LIQUID MESSAGES

The bodily fluids transport "messages" throughout the body: the blood, lymph, cerebro-spinal and interstitial fluids all cue the body as to its general state through the quality of the substances carried in their liquid medium. If they are sluggish and burdened down with toxic debris, the body will experience itself in a state of disrepair.

One of the ways I have always perceived cancer in people is that the fluids of their body become straw-colored. Perhaps this opaque color is caused by an extra abundance of waste materials released as the cells reproduce themselves at such an abnormal rate. If one could clear the fluids, the condition would not only be improved, but possibly reversed.

You can look into these fluids with your psychic awareness and get a strong message about how you are. This is preventive medicine at its best. By checking in to see what messages are being circulated, you can greatly influence your body to stay healthy and **ageless.** If you see the liquids as clear, full of electricity and sparkling with life, imprint to your body to continue exactly in that way by praising it and fixing the image of this clear flow in the mind of the cell. If not, you can completely wash away the negative potential before it becomes anything tangible by bringing your consciousness inside you and visioning or feeling that water is cascading through every particle of your being.

Lets try it! Take a moment and close your eyes. Imagine that you are looking at the fluids of your body. Simply ask your body to show you the various fluids. You can call them by name: "Show me the blood," or "Show me the lymph" and so on. Notice if they seem clear or murky. If they are dull or lifeless, interject the command that they be rejuvenated and visualize them as crystal clear and vibrant! After you do this, drink a glass of water with the command that it will enter and wash away anything not clear and pure. You'll be amazed how energized you feel.

THE BRAIN

How one interprets reality is very dependent on the quality of brain patterns which are either smooth flowing pulses, or chaotic, jammed channels, too filled with debris to support cohesive motion. The brain itself is over 90% water and is fed by the cerebro-spinal fluid that washes through and around it. Knowing this can help you to be motivated in terms of keeping your brain fluids clear. At the Light Institute, each series of sessions includes a cranial. The cranial is a highly sensitive work that re-aligns all the bones and sutures of the head and literally washes the brain by pumping the cerebro-spinal fluids. This activates the master glands and opens the consciousness by stimulating the pineal gland.

The water of the brain and nervous system is the most highly structured water in the body and is very sensitive to external electric and magnetic fields. It is important for you to know that the extremely low frequency (ELF) waves put out by your TV, hair dryer, computer and other household gadgets are very likely disrupting your brain fluids by altering or even destroying the crystalline colloids that maintain the structured water, and thus the life force of the brain.

THE SENSITIVITY OF WATER

Innumerable studies have been done to demonstrate that water is psychically sensitive. The classical study that has been repeated over and over again is that of energizing one container of water and then using it, as well as a container of untreated control water, to feed seedlings with each of the two waters to see if one or the other will cause better growth. The treated water always produces faster and more healthy growth in the young plants. What is the source of treatment? Usually nothing more than holding one container of water in the hands, to "energize" it. Some studies have shown that even gazing on the water can do the same thing. If you can make plants grow by just focusing on water, why not use this same technique to dissolve tumors, stimulate your endocrine glands, or clear your brain!

TRANSMUTING WATER

This is a test you can give yourself. Take a little drink of water to discover its taste. Then put your hand over the glass and see if you can feel anything. If it has a lot of minerals, or some pollutants such as chlorine, or radiation that is seeping into the soils around the world, you may feel a little electrical *zzzst*, or buzz. Leave your hand there until you feel either a cool wind or the buzz stops. This means that you have been able to transmute that energy and align it to your own frequency. Now take another drink. You will find that the water tastes differently; usually it tastes sweeter. Sunlight also influences water by activating its life force.

THE HUMAN DOWSING ROD

The fluidity of water can teach us that we are not solid, immobile beings, but rather ever-changing yet powerful channels of life. The water signs of astrology -- Cancer, Pisces and Scorpio attribute many of their unique gifts to the properties of their fluid element. Those aspects of the deepest secrets of the human psyche are immersed in the medium of water, which is the conduit of consciousness. Water as a liquid medium is one of the best conductors of energy which can actually be directed by our consciousness to increase our health and vitality.

This coherent liquid system within us can also act as a conveyor of information that relates and orients us to outside information. Through the function of "dowsing," our inner waters can tune us in to currents that are moving around us in our world. For example, one can find water by shifting the consciousness of the inner fluids to resonate to those of underground water currents.

I have found that nearly everyone can successfully dowse with a little practice. Even children (around 5 years old) can accomplish this as soon as they are big enough to hold the dowsing rods. In fact, a much higher percentage of children than adults can dowse, perhaps because their intuitive, flowing consciousness is still intact. Though dowsers are often very subjectively convinced that they can only dowse with a certain kind of dowsing rods, the truth is that the dowsing faculty is coming from the body, not the rods. The rods simply make the motion more visible so that the dowser can easily confirm the answer to the question.

Once the inner waters are focused on the goal, the dowser can actually dowse for any information being sought, whether it is pipe lines, gold, lost items or people and even blocks in one's own body. Many people use the pendulum over the body to better confirm and visualize the energy flows. The distance at which the auric flow travels from the body can be perceived by the use of a pendulum held at varying distances until it no longer swings with the auric current.

I have often used a pendulum to demonstrate how the auric field literally stops swinging in front of the throat when someone is smoking. I am well aware that understanding how damaging an addictive substance is has little affect on the need to continue using it. However, smoking is definitely related to the theme of hiding, or not allowing the heart to speak one's truth. So many of us have felt the pain of silence in our lives and it is very impressive when the pendulum stops dead still in front of the throat when someone is sucking smoke into their lungs. At the very least it allows us to embark upon some profound discussions relating to what is being held inside and what the price is to keep it there.

The pendulum responds to life, to the motion and pulse of electromagnetic currents that inform you about the quality of life force within and around you. Some sources say that the average human body has 90,000 volts of electricity per cubic centimeter. The electrical potential of all organs and systems in your body is charged by the fluid which must carry that electrical potential to the cellular level. Thus the life force aspect of water becomes of major concern. If you want to be healthy and **ageless**, you must bring water, the source of life, into your body so that it can rejuvenate and regenerate you.

* See **Elixir of the Ageless** by Patrick Flanagan and Gael Crystal Flanagan. *Vortex press 1986*

** **Water Wise** *by John W. Lauffer*

NOURISHING YOUR AGELESS BODY

"The foods we eat are not only vital because the nutrients they bring support our physical bodies, but they affect us emotionally, spiritually and psychically as well."

In today's world, the quantity of information we receive about the kind of food we should eat seems like an insurmountable barrage. Most people simply cannot attempt to decipher between the hype of advertisement and the elementary truth of the body's needs. We have an attitude that children must eat to grow and that once grown, somehow the food we eat is merely for our pleasure. We consequently eat too much and we do not eat well.

EATING EMOTIONALLY

Tragically, we eat too much because of an emotional need that perhaps began in childhood, through our body's direct association between being fed and feeling loved. As we move on into adulthood, we are expected to nourish ourselves, although we continue the habits and motives of eating that we learned in childhood. Thus, we eat in defiance, for comfort, and even for protection.

Our eating is often disconnected from the actual messages coming from our bodies as to what foods are necessary to maintain it in health and in an **ageless** state. Far too much emphases has been placed on foods that damage our bodies, rather than what foods should be taken in accordance with each body's particular balance and necessities. Though the human body is to some degree a predictable system of specific parts and general necessities, each body is absolutely unique. What would be a normal food for one body might be an allergen or reactive substance to another. The protein needs of one person may be entirely different than another. What would maintain good health in one body might cause arthritis in another due to an incapacity to transmute excess uric acid. Some people simply cannot digest proteins in the morning and are much better off with only fruit.

Another example of your body's uniqueness is how often you should eat. While some bodies may do well on two meals a day into adulthood, other bodies become severely hypoglycemic (low blood sugar) if they are not nourished every three hours or so. There have been some interesting studies that suggest more frequent meals, of equal caloric intake as a three meal a day plan, may lower cholesterol by influencing insulin levels that affect the ability of the liver to synthesize cholesterol.

You might find it fascinating to observe for a week your own rhythm so that you could begin to know some of your body's basic requirements. If you would simply notice how often and at what times in the day you begin to feel tired or irritable, very quickly you will discover an emerging pattern of food frequency needed by your own body. It will probably help you to write it down so that you have a comprehensive survey.

LISTENING TO YOUR BODY

Though we will discuss in this chapter some nutrients that have shown themselves to strengthen or maintain adult bodies, before you can truly utilize the information relative to yourself, you must learn the intuitive capacity to commune with your own body. What has been determined good for the body has been taken over by the mind so that the tendency is to "think" about what to put into the body rather than finding out from the body what it needs or wants. The body functions through a complex orchestration of assimilating and combining raw materials to create specific substances necessary for perfect health. It knows exactly what it needs at any given moment.

Today there are technologies that can analyze the elements present in the body and then deduct what substances need to be taken in, often at great cost and effort. In truth, you can do this for yourself every bit as well or even better than a machine can. The only thing necessary is to simply and clearly ask your body what it is looking for, and it will give you the answer. If you focus your attention on some item of food and ask your body, " Should I eat this?" you will either hear a yes or no answer, or you will feel an intuitive response that confirms a sense of what your body wants. "Intuiting" your body is a powerful informational system that will not fail you and is easy to learn.

These intuitive techniques are extremely valuable, not only in terms of what you should eat, but also in terms of the vitamin and other supplements that might be taken into the body at any given time. For example, there are helpful bacteria in the intestines that manufacture B vitamins. As long as the "flora and the fauna" of the intestinal tract has not been depleted by stress or adverse activity, supplementation of these crucial vitamins may not be necessary. It is even possible that your body will stop synthesizing them if you constantly over supply them in supplementary form. At other times these supplements will do much to protect the body from undue stress. Therefore, I continually ask my body on a daily basis which supplements I should take so that my body has the opportunity to reject anything that is not useful for the moment.

THE PENDULUM AND FOOD

Sometimes when you begin to learn this intuitive language of communication with your body, you may not be sure if you are clear enough or whether you are just imagining. One way to become more trusting is to use a pendulum for verification of appropriate food intake at any given time. Though I have used pendulums almost all of my life to find things or check body energies, I had never considered their use in terms of food until I witnessed the application of this most valuable technique by William Teller from the Stanford University department of physical sciences. Many years ago at the annual Edgar Cayce medical symposium he demonstrated the use of a pendulum to ascertain if a certain food or other substance would be tolerated by an individual. It was very clear that there was great variation in how different bodies responded to the same foods; one substance was appropriate for one person and absolutely toxic for another. This was most often the case when foods contained sugar or other chemical properties.

It is very helpful to have something that gives you a yes or a no answer and a physical signal confirming your intuitive choice when you are first exploring the notion of talking to your body. Because the pendulum activates a relationship between your nervous system and your body consciousness, it will swing or move without your overt control. It is a most amazing sensation to hold something weighted on a string and feel it moving by itself as you lightly dangle it over your food!

You will find it fascinating to practice and also to see which of the foods you normally eat the body would rather not have forced upon it. After you have gained mastery over the pendulum, you can be equally effective in gathering this information by simply placing your hand over the food and asking your body, "Shall I eat this or shall I eat that?" You will discover that you can receive very clear mandates from your body in terms of any question you ask it.

ALLERGIES

Considering the individuality of bodies, it is not surprising that so many people suffer from allergies. Imagine how this can happen in a family where everyone is served the same food and yet some of it may only be well-tolerated by a few of them. I discovered this dilemma with my little tribe of six children, some of whom could not stomach eggs, others who were allergic to wheat, and so on. Conquering allergies is very important to the **Ageless Body** because the overall effect is loss of energy and malaise that set up a negative attitude towards life. Allergies lead to life in the "grey zone" and if you feel tired and hopeless about life, you simply will be creating a scenario for aging.

Since food allergies are present in early infancy, it would be fantastic if parents could be taught to check which foods to give their babies right from the beginning of eating solid foods. This is a story babies should tell, not standardized medicine. Whole lifetimes of misery could be avoided in this way. I'll never forget my darling Megan pouncing on her chocolate cake at her first birthday party. Nor will I ever forget the three months of terrible skin rashes that followed!

TECHNIQUES FOR FOOD TESTING

There are several ways to check for food allergies. In fact, it is a good idea to use these techniques not only to find out what you shouldn't eat, but what you should eat and when. They are very helpful for checking the frequency and choice of food supplements too.

First and most simple is to use a pendulum either over

the food while asking if it is good for you, or even over a list of foods that you normally eat to see if any of them could be causing trouble.

Another kinesthetic way to test is by making a circle with your right thumb and forefinger and then reaching your left forefinger into the circle and connecting it to your left thumb. You now have two interconnected circles. Ask mentally if something is good for you and simultaneously pull your two circles apart in an attempt to separate them. If the answer is a yes, they will not pull apart, even with your effort. If the answer is no, you will find that they will separate. Try it!

My son Bapu enjoys the standard kinesthetic test in which he touches or holds something in his left hand while extending out his right arm with clinched fist facing down towards the floor. Then I command his arm to "resist" while I press down just above the wrist. It is important to do the resist test first to determine how much strength there is in the arm, and then place the item in question in the left hand and ask again. If the substance is good for him, his arm will not yield much to my pressing, but if it is bad for him, it will weaken him and his arm will move down towards his side with my pressure. It is great fun to do these tests with your children as a creative way to avoid always saying no to candy or other things you know they should not eat. This way you are not the "bad guy" that they rebel against by eating what you tell them not to eat.

Another interesting way to check your body's reaction to food is by feeling your pulse. When you place something in your mouth that your body doesn't like, your pulse will immediately speed up. You don't have to know anything special about pulses to do this test. Just turn your left arm and hand up towards the ceiling and bring your right hand under your wrist, grabbing your left arm at the wrist with the four fingers of your right hand. You will be able to feel your pulse right away. Use your middle finger to press down for the pulse and lift the other fingers up lightly so that you are focused in one position. This is the position of the liver, according to Chinese pulse diagnosis.

Count each beat of the pulse during fifteen seconds and then multiply it by four. This will tell you how many beats you have in one minute. It is important to feel the pulse for a few seconds before you start counting as you may need to settle into your rhythm. Also, you should be sitting down. Now place a tiny piece of the food in question, under your tongue. (Experiment with bread crumbs, as wheat is a common allergen. Try cheese, sugar, meat, eggs and so on). After placing the food in your mouth, wait about two minutes and take your pulse again. You will be shocked to find that your pulse has risen by as much as twenty to thirty beats if you are allergic to the substance.

FOOD PREPARATION

The foods we eat are not only vital because the nutrients they bring support our physical bodies, but they affect us emotionally, spiritually and psychically as well. The best of food offered by someone in a hurry or resentful of preparing it will create the energy of indigestion and be unassimilated by the body. Food and its preparation are the offering to life itself. It can not be underestimated how important it is that food be prepared and received joyfully. If you are the one that prepares food for your family, and as you make dinner your thoughts are still caught up in the struggles of your daily occupation, your entire family will suffer the result. Therefore, your capacity to turn your entire attention to the preparation of the food is crucial to your family.

I recommend drinking water and washing your face when you return home from work to clear your energy from the residues of problems and work related anxieties. Even if you have been home all day, it is useful to create a special mood when you are going to prepare a meal. Spinning around and following with a few moments meditation will help you to concentrate and be present with the task. Playing music is also a great way to get into a giving mode. Many people feel that cooking, chopping vegetables, arranging food and even washing dishes are all forms of meditation, and indeed they can be if the intention is there. Most of all, the preparation and consumption of food needs to be a creative and delightful event for **you!**

ENERGIZING YOUR FOOD

Not only should food be lovingly prepared, but you can even do more to insure that it is in concert with what your body can digest and utilize. Since your body sends out electromagnetic energies, you can align the food you eat with your own energies to receive the maximum benefit from your food. Just as you did in energizing your water, place your hands over your plate of food and feel the energies.

A quick way to learn these radiating energies is to place your hands over something with chocolate or sugar in it. Try a chocolate cake, or chocolate ice cream and you will immediately be able to perceive the buzz coming from these volatile substances.

As you place your hands over your food, you will not only be removing anything out of sync with your body, but you will be energizing it so that it is the most beneficial to you.

FASTING

Fasting is a subject that causes a lot of controversy. On the one hand, there can be no argument that the toxic impurities which build up in our organs, tissues and interstitial spaces contribute to the aging process. Fasting serves very well to clean out the body so that it does not become overburdened with debris to the extent that it no longer functions with precision. Because water is the great detoxifier, it plays a major role in any bodily clean-up project. But fasting need not be something so severe as prolonged water fasts that necessitate supervision by experienced professionals. It can also be an opportunity for the body to rest itself from dietary overload, poor food combinations and other injustices we heap upon it through our ignorance.

Short fasts with either fortified water or juices can be very helpful to the body. An excellent fasting water is one with a small amount of pure maple syrup and lemon juice added to the pure water. Unless I am traveling I give my body a reprieve from eating one day a week with freshly made juices that rest and nourish it at the same time. It feels good to do and it is very energizing. If you decide to try this kind of fasting, be careful to make your juices only from organic fruits and vegetables.

Some studies have shown that reduced metabolism from semi-starvation diets increase longevity. One of the things I like best about my one-day-a-week liquid diet is that it keeps me from eating large meals during the rest of the week. With only liquid in the digestive tract, the stomach soon shrinks so that I feel full on much less food.

DIET

Everyone asks what is the best diet for the **Ageless Body** and whether they should be vegetarian or not. Each body is so uniquely different that you must explore with your body which foods and style of eating is best for you. The earlier in life you do this for yourself and for your children, the healthier you will be. There are bodies that require some consumption of flesh for certain periods, while others would be horribly disrupted and contaminated by such a practice.

Eating preference is very much the habit of emotional and societal orientation. If you could look at it from a global perspective, you would immediately realize that as a whole, humans definitely need to stop eating meat because the valuable land used up feeding animals could be much more productively utilized for crop production and pharmaceuticals. There would be enough food to feed the world and erase hunger from human experience if we would use our intelligence rather than our gluttonous tastes to nourish ourselves as a collective group. In the future, more value will be placed on fluids as a source of nourishment and they will be impregnated with life force elements. One of the best things you can do for yourself is to use lemon water at the table. Lemons help the liver to purify the body and they are the natural food source of bio-elemental lithium. Through its capacity to transmute elements, lithium is crucial to the overall energy balance of your body.

Eating cooked and dead life forms is not the most healthful diet for a living body. Changing denatured proteins, whose molecules have been altered by the cooking process back into their component amino acids so that the body can reconstruct the specific enzymes and hormones it needs, is the long way around. We do not yet fully understand the "synergy" of Mother Nature. Any one food has many different attributes that work together to produce the quality and life force of the whole. When we alter our food, we have usually not only destroyed some of the elements, but we have removed the way they compliment each other, leaving something which may react in a totally different way within our bodies.

Perhaps as much an issue of what we eat is the quality of what we eat. All meat fed to us from supermarkets in today's world is full of the impurities of growth hormones, antibiotics and other stimulants fed to animals kept in unnatural spaces. The adrenaline and fear released into the muscle tissue at the time the animal was killed may be influencing the amount of fear that we carry around in our daily lives. None of this is conducive to heath within our bodies. Even the vegetables eaten today carry with them the danger of inorganic fertilizers, pesticides and other chemical and toxic sprays that, once taken into our own systems, continually create compounds the liver is unable to dissolve or rid from the body.

All of this teaches us to perceive food beyond its mere presentation. A lovely looking carrot filled with toxic agents may be completely denatured and lacking in the vitamins and minerals it is touted to contain because the soil in which it was grown has been utterly depleted. Only your intuitive sense will tell you if it will deliver what a carrot is supposed to contain.

The **Ageless Body** needs "living" food to sustain itself in perfect balance. If you really care about your body, you must structure your diet so that at least 1/3 of your food intake is alive. You can easily do this if you eat sprouts everyday and drink freshly made juices. Every city apartment could have a sprouting jar on the table.

SUPER FOODS

There is a fascinating array of new products and super foods that can help the body to maintain an **ageless** homeostasis of health. Here are a few of my favorites:

BLUE-GREEN ALGAE

One of my favorite super foods is blue-green algae. It is a micro-organism of unparalleled significance to the future of humanity. Micro-algae is a complete food that contains all the essential amino acids for protein synthesis and production of hormones and enzymes. Amino acids are also the components of neurotransmitters that are responsible for intelligent brain activity and function. These are very important qualities because one of the worst side-effects of aging is the loss of memory and mental clarity.

Most important to me is the fact that algae have been living on this planet for millions of years and have adapted themselves through all the atmospheric changes Earth has experienced. In early times, for example, there was no ozone layer to protect life forms from the sun's radiation. The algae, living on the surface of the water, developed attributes that protected it from the immense quantities of radiation present. As our ozone layers thin and our own meddling with radioactive substances cause us to again find need of protection from radiation, we can turn to the algae who solved the dilemma by producing large quantities of beta-carotene.

Beta-carotene can now protect us just as well from the ever increasing amount of radiation and other atmospheric pollutants threatening our health. It is a very effective tumor fighter that wards off any number of carcinogens entering our bodies from our polluted environment.

Another important attribute of blue-green algae is that it is one of the highest sources of chlorophyll. Chlorophyll is chemically very similar to the hemoglobin, or red blood cells, that nourish our bodies.

Best of all is the fact that blue-green algae is a food that is ecologically renewable. It grows in mineral-rich aquatic environments where it replenishes itself on a daily basis.

Because of its "soft" cell wall, blue-green algae is easily assimilated by the body. It seems so much more intelligent to provide the body with amino acids rather than proteins that must be broken down into amino acids, assimilated and then reconstituted.

When I travel with the children, we always carry blue-green algae with us so that I know they are getting their nutritional requirements no matter where we are in the world. I like the small flavored clumps that are like treats for the children, as well as capsulated or powder forms so that I have several ways to serve it.

When you first begin to consume these super foods it is important to start slowly. If you take too much blue-green algae, you will trigger a detoxification process. Thus, it is better to take small amounts and build up to what feels like a sustaining quantity that allows you plenty of energy without forcing too much cleansing of the body.

SEA VEGETABLES

Another form of algae are the macroscopic marine algae known as sea vegetables. You might be familiar with them as kelp or dulse. I feel they are one of the most important foods of today and the future, because of their fantastic ability to protect against environmental pollutants and radiation.

The sodium alienate found in kelp is the best protector against strontium-90 coming from fallout of nuclear power plants. Dulce is a red sea vegetable that binds plutonium, thus protecting from its absorption into the body. Sea vegetables provide essential vitamins, minerals and natural iodine. This is of great importance to you because of its effect on the thyroid gland that regulates your energy levels. Chlorinated tap water leaches iodine from the thyroid gland, causing imbalances that greatly influence aging. Natural iodine is crucial to protect you from the radioactive iodine-131 released by nuclear power plant emissions.

One of the main reasons I eat sea vegetables is their power to dissolve fat and mucus deposits. I must confess that my body tends to store fat and so I place a lot of emphasis in my diet on those substances that help me to dissolve and release these unwanted deposits.

NUTRITIONAL YEAST

Nutritional yeast is another super food that generously supports the **Ageless Body**. People are afraid of it because of the increase in fungus and yeast infestations (such as Candida Albicans) that have become such a problem. It is very important to understand that nutritional yeast is a particular species of yeast (*Saccharomyces cerevisiae*) that is completely different from the Candida Albicans species of negative organisms. The susceptibility to such organisms has to do with the lack of beneficial bacteria that keep the flora of the intestines in balance so that other toxic organisms cannot take control. However, if you already suffer from candidiasis I would recommend that you ask your body if you should take any forms of yeast, before trying them. A prominent German researcher, Holger Metz, has shown that *Saccharomyces cerevisiae* protects humans from many of the results of radiation damage such as skin redness, loss of hair and blood disorders. Nutritional yeast also protects us from the toxic effects of pollutants including heavy metals, carbon monoxide, DDT and lead poisoning.

It is a shame to cast nutritional yeast into the valley of doom when it offers so much incredible energy to the body.

Nutritional yeast contains such a powerful complement of essential amino acids that a small amount will satisfy the body's protein requirements. It also has what is called " the life-force factor" which activates the body and makes you feel so much more energetic. If you have trouble with your blood sugar balance, the chromium in nutritional yeast will greatly aid in the normalization of glucose levels.

Nutritional yeast is a wonderful "pick me up" in the afternoon. If you put it in water or juice you will feel its effects in about ten or fifteen minutes. Sprinkled on food, it helps to protect the balance of nutrients taken into the body so that the necessary amino acids are present in the meal. This is very important in a vegetarian diet when food combination must be exact enough to supply the essential amino acid building blocks. You must be sure that you are taking calcium and magnesium because the yeast is high in phosphorus which uses them to be metabolized. Nutritional yeast also has large quantities of B vitamins, often including B_{12}, which so influences the energy of the body. Begin with about one-half teaspoon and slowly build up to two tablespoons taken in several dosages during the day.

SUPER SUPPLEMENTS

There are several supplemental substances that can really make a difference to your **Ageless Body.** You have probably read about the many vitamin and mineral supplements available to protect your body so I won't review them, but there are some new advancements that deserve special attention:

L-GLUTAMINE

L-glutamine is one of my favorite supplements because it is so helpful to the brain. Glucose and glutamic acid are the only two substances that actually fuel the brain. However, there is a problem because glutamic acid is restricted by the brain barrier and very little dietary glutamic acid is successful at arriving at the gray matter where it can be converted to a compound that regulates brain cell activity. Fortunately L-glutamine, the amid form of glutamic acid, can cross the barrier and is converted into glutamic acid.

L-glutamine feeds the brain and therefore prevents hypoglycemia, fatigue and depression, and has been used successfully to treat impotence and senility; it reportedly increases intelligence. I give L-glutamine to my children to keep them from craving sweets and I have used it for many years to help people with alcohol problems.

AMINO ACIDS

Amino acids can be among the best proponents of the **Ageless Body.** Certain amino acids exhibit an incredible influence over the pituitary gland that releases Growth Hormone to repair cells. Growth Hormone tells the body to burn fat and build muscle as well as activates the immune system. After the age of about twenty-six, your body's production of Growth Hormone begins to decrease.

Amino acids arginine and ornithine boost Growth Hormone release. I take a preparation of these and other amino acids especially balanced to provide optimum GH production. They must be taken on an empty stomach to avoid being digested as food, rather than being sent directly to the pituitary for activation of GH. Since the pituitary normally releases GH at night, before bed is a good time to take them if you haven't eaten for at least 4 hours. I often take them in the morning, wait at least 1 hour before eating and do two minutes of peak exercise that stimulates the pituitary to release its GH.   GH is a powerful way to maintain a healthy body and keep weight in check, but you must do some research for yourself to make sure you are in accordance with your body's needs.*

PYCNOGENOL

Pycnogenol is a powerful bioflavonoid that boosts vitamin C to protect and build the collagen of the body. The integrity of collagen is essential for the strength of blood vessels and capillaries and even the wrinkling of the skin. If you bruise easily you are probably in need of this wonderful gift from nature that comes from the bark of the European coastal pine, Pinus Martima. Pycnogenol protects you from bruising which is important because bruises allow free radicals to damage and destroy cells. Free radicals cause many of the degenerative conditions associated with aging.

ANTIOXIDANTS

Free radicals are unstable atoms that bombard and destroy the protective membranes of cells in the body due to their insatiable need to oxidize anything they come into contact with. Free radicals are so destructive that they can actually alter the DNA and RNA functioning of the cell. This is very important to you because the vitality of your cellular body is the measure of your agelessness. I feel that future study will show free radicals as the major cause of aging.

Antioxidants are the heroes of your body's defense against free radicals because they protect molecules and tissues from oxidation.   There is so much written on antioxidants that I will only name some of most powerful ones so you can check to see if you are getting them into you body: Beta-carotene, A, C, E, B, PYCNOGENOL, PABA, minerals SELENIUM, ZINC and the amino acid CYSTEINE.

ORGANIC GERMANIUM

There can be no question but that oxygen is one of the great supporters of life and since the functioning of our cellular body depends on its sufficient availability, those substances that protect oxygen in our body are of great value to us. Besides the antioxidants, there is another substance that is key to oxygen take-up in the body.

Organic germanium (Ge-132) not only stimulates oxygen function but boosts the immune system as well. It was first synthesized by the Japanese researcher Dr. F. Kazuhiko Asai in 1967 and is taken by over six million Japanese a day. Ge-132 has a powerful chelating capacity and so binds heavy metals, some types of ionizing radiation, and other poisons. It also has been found to be an anti-cancer agent.

MEMBRANE COMPLEX

Dr. Hans Nieper engendered a breakthrough formula that creates a protective process in the membrane of the cell. It is called Membrane Complex and has been used to aid degenerative diseases for more that twenty-five years. Membrane Complex is composed of essential mineral components combined with 2-AEP (two-aminoethyl phosphoric acid). 2-AEP is a neurotransmitter found in cellular membranes that activates an electrical charge which protects the cell membrane from invasion by toxins and viruses. According to Dr. Nieper, the body has 90,000 volts of electricity per cubic centimeter. This was an exciting discovery for me because I feel that the electrical quality of the body is crucial to the spark of life and very much influences the strength of the auric field that determines the **Ageless Body.**

2-AEP carries minerals to the lipid pore sites where substances move in and out of the cell. The lack of cell membrane integrity is a major factor in succumbing to illness and degeneration on the cellular level. Here is a great boost to the immune system that must remain strong if aging is to be conquered.

FEEDING YOUR IMMUNE SYSTEM

Nothing could be more important to the perpetuation of a healthy, **Ageless Body** than a strong immune system. The thymus gland, spleen, lymph nodes and ducts, bone marrow, and various chemical substances such as growth hormone, antibodies and interferon comprise the immune system. The thymus instructs the white blood cells called "T cells" what to attack and when. The T cells also have a hand in the formation of antibodies. If the thymus is weak, the T cells may even attack your own body's cells rather than recognizing the bacteria, viruses and cancerous cells that should be their targets.

It is the weakening of the immune system that signals aging. This begins after puberty when the all important immune manufacturer, the thymus gland, begins to shrivel in size, thus reducing its functioning capacities. Fortunately there are several nutrients that have been shown to actually increase the size of the thymus gland and boost its functioning: vitamin A, E, C, minerals zinc and selenium, and the amino acid cysteine.

To keep your defense system strong, your body requires that you give it the raw materials it needs to manufacture the substances which will not only fight off attacking viruses and other organisms, but that will also boost its life force energy. Other herbs and preparations for your immune system include: garlic, ginger, ginseng, echinachia root, lecithin, bee pollen, lithium and palo arco.

Acupuncture is one of the best systems of medicine to support the immune system. Traditionally, acupuncture was used as preventative medicine and the practitioner was considered a failure if his patients actually succumbed to disease. If the meridian system is kept in a balanced state and the energy (chi) flows throughout all its prescribed channels, the body will be strong enough to defend itself against any invasion. Auricular or ear acupuncture is especially effective because it stimulates the organs of the body. Our body is under so much attack by environmental pollutants that you must maintain contact with your immune system at all times. This does not need to provoke feelings of anxiety, but rather an intelligent and intuitive attention to your body. By checking with your body, you can discover which substances your body needs at any given time.

Your immune system offers you a chance to review your commitment to your physical body. Some people wander around in their bodies without ever really being present in them at all. The diseases relevant on the planet today -- cancer, AIDS and radiation poisoning -- have one major theme or message: Presence in body. In each of them the cells cannot maintain their integrity or identity because there is no strong conscious focus. For example, cancer cells forget their purpose and randomly multiply, AIDS viruses attack weakened immune systems with no defense forces protecting the body, and the free radicals produced by radiation tear their way past the membranes of the cell to destroy its core. Your consciousness is the integrating and protecting factor that reminds the cells about who they are.

All this vulnerability must pose the question to humanity to remember its own purpose for being. When you have a sense of your purpose, you are much more powerful with the force of your energy. Communing with your immune system can greatly affect its functioning. Practicing the color exercise of feeding your endocrine system (The Endocrine Secret chapter) with extra emphasis on the thymus and spleen, as well as scanning your white cell activity to see that cells are functioning properly and not confusing enemies with your own molecules, will give your body the message that you are present and caring for its well being. The body will not go on indefinitely without your conscious input.

BREATH, THE BEST FOOD OF ALL

As you have seen how important oxygen is to the health of your cells, you become aware that one of the most important things you can do to gain an **Ageless Body** is to breathe. You may never have considered breathing as the greatest nourishment available to you and yet it is true. The pattern of your breath reflects your emotional and physiological states. Conscious breathing can change the entire physiological rhythm of your body, restoring tired muscles, feeding the cells and even gently massaging your vital organs.

There are actually three lobes of the lungs that are fed by different breathing patterns or levels. Many people only breathe from the top lobe, which feeds the bronchi by a rapid, shallow breath, rather than the middle and lower lobes that bring the breath down to the abdomen.

All too often, the newborn baby breathes in with a startle reflex, and never really learns to breathe deep breaths with even inhalation and exhalation. It is just as important to exhale as it is to inhale because with your out-breath goes the carbon dioxide and stale energies that the body needs to release. Many people find it harder to take a long out-breath than to inhale. Try it now and see if this is true for you.

FIRE BREATH

The most powerful breathing technique I know is an exercise called the fire breath, a form of Pranayama. Prana is the term for the life force energy attached to the oxygen in the air we breathe. I do this exercise every morning to push out the old breath so that I can really breathe fresh energy into my body. Do this just one to three times in the beginning and you will be amazed how energized you feel.

Sit with your spine straight so that the energies in your body can move up and down without hindrance. Either close your fists grabbing onto your thumb, or place your thumb and forefinger together. This creates an energetic arc so that your energy is circled throughout your body.

Begin to "snort" or exhale forcibly and slowly out of your nose. Imagine that you are pretending to be a choo-choo train and increase the snorts to make the train sounds. Continue with very fast snorts for a few successions and then slow back down to a stop. You will notice that as you snort, you are pushing down with your diaphragm into the belly. At first you may need a tissue near by as there may be a lot of mucus in your nose.

When you finish the fire breath, breathe in deeply, and as you exhale, squeeze your anus up tightly. This tightens the pubicoccxygeous muscle that runs through the perineum area. Squeezing closes off an important acupuncture point so that energy does not drain out from below, but rather moves up the body, nourishing the higher centers of consciousness.

Take several normal breaths and begin again. This is a perfect way to begin a meditation because it helps the mind to let go of the body and allows the spiritual energy to flow through.

Now begin to breathe deep breaths all the way down to your belly. Focus on drawing the life force of prana into your body and concentrating on this act of nourishing yourself.

Breath is a powerful interface between the physical and spiritual worlds. It also is directly tied to the Emotional Body that so influences your self-worth and joy in life. If you are willing to bring your breath onto a conscious level, you will be giving yourself a clear message of your intention to use life fully and attain an **Ageless Body**.

An excellent work on GH is "Life Extension " by Durk Pearson and Sandy Shaw.

THE ENDOCRINE SECRET

*"The endocrine system is the major key to the **Ageless Body**."*

The endocrine glands of your body regulate your metabolism and therefore are crucial to your sense of well being and your level of energy. The endocrine system is the major key to the **Ageless Body.** Not only is it the source of the operative juices that give the body its metabolic instructions, but it is one of the great thresholds between the invisible worlds that source life, and the physical world of matter that expresses it. The chakric vortexes express life force on an energetic level, and the endocrines express that same energy on a physical level.

The chakras influence the endocrines to carry out the energy balance as it is available through the will. It may surprise you to consider that staying alive and healthy requires you to consciously and unconsciously choose it. How old you look and feel is directly related to the source of energy in the chakras. If you want to create an **Ageless Body**, you must "will" energy into your body by concentrating on the endocrines.

The correlation between vitality and the endocrines expresses a relationship of intrinsic energy resource that is more than just the physiology of hormonal secretion. Hormonal effects are more subtle than can be measured by science on a strictly biological basis.

The hormonally rich liquids secreted directly into the

bloodstream or the blood vessels of organs, carry the energy of life into the body. Hormones produced and secreted by the endocrine system literally govern the quality of bodily functions and its response to life. Such diverse and major processes as growth and development; reproduction; maintenance of electrolyte, water and nutrient balance of the blood; regulation of cellular metabolism and energy balance, as well as mobilization of body defenses against stressors, are all under control of the endocrines.

The effectiveness of hormonal control on the body is mitigated by many variables which alter the endocrine functions. Acute and chronic non-endocrine illnesses, body composition, weight and diet, medications and drugs, nervous system activity and stress, as well as sleep-wake cycles and levels of physical activity, all play havoc with the endocrines' ability to deliver life force to your body.

The hormones secreted by the endocrine glands are directed toward "target" cells to accomplish their designated tasks. Within the cells are protein receptors who must be active and alert to receive the secretions. Receptors respond to hormone binding by prompting the cell to perform, or "turn on" some genetically determined function.

The sensitivity of the receptors diminishes with age,

even though the hormonal levels of the endocrine gland may appear constant. As the chakric vortexes slow down, the transmission of pure energy from ethereal to physical levels diminishes and the body reflects the decrease by closing down. This seems to be the microcosmic story all over again. Why does the cell become desensitized? Why does it choose not to receive the "juice?" Even on these cellular levels, the unconscious will gives up the fight and turns off life.

This is where you can influence the direction of the body by using consciousness to encourage the receptivity of the cell. When you command the cells to receive energy, they will be excited by the biochemical messages and take up the carriers that return them to their timeless state of vitality. The way to command them is by communicating via the language of energy. To the cells this is a perceptual communique such as visualization, in which you send them a light frequency that excites them.

Try this exercise: Close your eyes and breathe in. As you breathe in, imagine a trillion miniature arrows, like pin pricks of light, piercing your body. As they touch you, suck in your breath with each wave of light pricks. Then breathe out normally and suck in again. Do this sucking breath stronger and stronger, several times, until you feel the lightness and energetic feeling that comes over your body.

ENDOCRINE FUNCTION

Though you could learn to alter your endocrine functioning by the simple focus of your attention without intellectually knowing anything specifically about them, you will find it quite interesting to discover something about what the different endocrine glands do for you. This will help your ability to concentrate on them and enhance your appreciation of this divine instrument we call the body.

Some of the endocrines are the actual glands of secretion while others are organs with endocrine functions. Though there are a fair number of them, we will focus primarily on seven which I feel are the most important to support your ageless state. We'll start at the bottom of our energy totem pole with the energies we most recognize.

1. SEXUAL ORGANS-GONADS

The gonads, or sexual glands, produce the hormones that direct the body in its procreational quest. Not only do they synthesize and secrete the essences for new life through the production of eggs and sperm, but they cause the body to desire sexual expression. It is a trickery of the body to stimulate the delicious sensations that cause you to seek sexual experience so that the body can reproduce itself. This is why females feel especially receptive sexually during ovulation, and certainly it is why the sexual drive changes its flavor when procreation is no longer a possibility.

Male and female hormonal balances definitely effect personality expression, and both men and women undergo cyclic swings of mood and feeling as their hormonal secretions irrupt and subside according to the needs and rhythms of the gonadal organs.

As hysterectomies have become a common habit of medical practice, the opportunity to evaluate the effect of loss of primary endocrine organs on subtle emotional levels, as well as physical levels, is painfully obvious. Women often suffer pangs of anxiety and depression even though they express relief from the worry of pregnancy. This emotional reaction is not one to be dismissed lightly as it stems from a deep-rooted aspect of the self in which the body identifies its life force in terms of all the characteristics of youthful reproductive potential. This can be balanced with consciousness as the woman learns to speak to her body via energy messages that serve the same identification function as did the organs themselves. Hormonal replacement helps to ease the symptoms and slow down what would be a rapid aging process. Without the hormones, the body deduces that it is time to age. Of course, there are still substantial risks, such as cancer, that occur with hormonal replacement, mostly because it is so difficult to deduce the appropriate dosage in a constantly changing biodynamic organism such as the human body.

2. ADRENALS

The adrenals are a pair of tiny glands situated one on top of each kidney. Besides producing more than a dozen corticosteroid hormones in the outer cortex layer, the inner medulla is functionally part of the sympathetic nervous system and supports our response to stress. The "flight or fight" reaction to stressors is reinforced and prolonged by the adrenals. While this was seemingly more immediate in our caveman days, our adrenals are overworked today because of our emotional and mental addiction to fear in so many aspects of our life. The tremendous amounts of anger we habitually indulge in cause us to trigger the adrenals on a dangerously regular basis.

Sore throats, heart palpitation, sweating, intense nervousness are just a few of the disadvantages of adrenal stress. Much more significant is the relationship between adrenal exhaustion and poor immunity. When the adrenals are working overtime because the mental and emotional bodies are responding to life as an emergency, the body simply cannot protect itself the way it should because its energy is bound up in cycles of over-response and exhaustion.

You can see by this scenario that the act of reinterpreting the world from an emergency perspective to a quiet place of observation could do a lot for prolonged and peaceful life. If you can dictate such an awareness to your body through your consciousness, instead of a burned out nervous system, you will promote an **Ageless Body!**

3. PANCREAS

The pancreas is essential in maintaining your energy balance through its control of the glucose or sugar levels of the blood. The opposing hormones, insulin and glucagon, work as a regulating team to insure the blood sugar balance

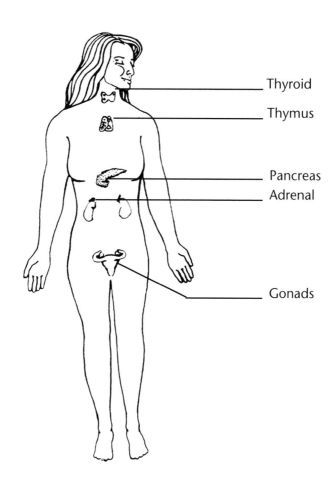

Thyroid

Thymus

Pancreas

Adrenal

Gonads

of your body. When you eat sugar, there is an immediate release of insulin to stop the liver from converting any more glycogen (stored energy) into glucose. However, the sugar energy is used up long before the insulin so that after about two hours there is a drop in the blood sugar level and you feel the irritability and weakness caused by hypoglycemia, or low blood sugar.

When the body begins to age, there is a temptation to consume increasing quantities of sugar, including alcohol, to compensate for the tired feelings of the body. This is a tragic mistake since the overloading of sugar stresses the pancreas and initiates a downward spiral of external dependency that exhausts the body's energy regulating mechanisms. A further disadvantage is that sucrose (table sugar) causes a sustained release of insulin in the bloodstream. Not only is there evidence that excessive insulin fosters arteriosclerosis, but it also interrupts the action of the immune system by suppressing the release of growth hormone. Since much of the secretion of growth hormone is released by the pituitary within the first hour and a half of sleep, no sugar should be consumed for several hours before bedtime lest the powerful growth hormones that stimulate the body to fight plaques, viruses, and repair the cells, be inhibited. SUGAR BEFORE BED INTERFERES WITH YOUR IMMUNE SYSTEM!

4. THYMUS

I have included the thymus gland because I feel that we will come to appreciate its effect on our overall state of being as further study is done on its functioning in the body. The thymus is the master gland of our immune system and therefore must receive alert attention, since our immune systems are so stressed in today's world. The thymus gland instructs certain white blood cells, called T cells, to attack a myriad of invading and destructive enemies such as viruses, bacteria and cancer cells. It is interesting that the thymic hormones are essential for the development of immune response and yet the thymus begins to shrivel at puberty, leaving the body with less and less capacity to respond to external threat. As you age, your T cells may not be able to distinguish between the enemy cells and those of your own body, which is what happens in autoimmune diseases like arthritis. You can reactivate and enlarge the thymus by taking certain nutrients such as vitamin C, A, E, minerals like zinc and selenium, and the amino acid cytosine. Check with your doctor or nutritionist for your individual doses.

The thymus influences a feeling of well-being. Eastern healers recommend a daily pounding over the breast bone to continue to stimulate the thymus. Bring all your fingers together and rapidly pound the area just below your right clavicle or collarbone, on the right side of the sternum.

5. THYROID-PARATHYROID

The thyroid gland is one of the largest endocrine glands in the body and releases two thyroid hormones called thyroxine and thyrocalcitonin, or thyroid hormone collectively. The thyroid governs the energy levels of the body through its control of the metabolic process. In fact, thyroid hormone affects virtually every cell in the body except the thyroid gland itself, the adult brain, spleen and gonads! If you want to feel energetic, you must pay attention to your thyroid.

The parathyroids are a pair of tiny glands embedded behind the thyroid which exert the single most control on the calcium balance of the blood through their release of PTH. Calcium balance is very much a part of the premenstrual syndrome, as well as nervous system activity. The PTH affects the ionic calcium levels by stimulating the skeleton, kidneys and intestine. Your nerve impulses, muscle contractions and blood clotting mechanisms are dependent on precise control of ionic calcium.

6. PITUITARY

The Pituitary gland is truly a master gland within your body. It secretes tropic hormones which stimulate other glands to secrete hormones, though its anterior lobe is influenced to do so by the hypothalamus. The anterior lobe is very important to us because of its secretion of growth hormone (GH). In the young, GH stimulates the long bone growth and increased muscle mass. "Build muscle, burn fat" is the motto of the GH. It decreases in the mid twenties resulting, for many of us, in weight gain. This is true because GH causes the cells to utilize fats for fuel in order to conserve glucose and also promotes protein synthesis. With its decrease, the fat storage increases, and even though you may engage in considerable exercise, your body just doesn't seem to burn the fat. GH has other important gifts for the body: it maintains homeostatic blood glucose levels by decreasing the rate of glucose uptake and metabolism.

This is of great importance to those who expend energy on psychic levels because the body must balance energy output for such demanding awareness with the more physical needs of the physiological body.

The pituitary puts out a whole slew of other regulating hormones that accomplish everything from controlling the gonads (ovaries and testes) and their myriad procreational functions, to the production of urine and water balances, to orchestrating the thyroid's release of thyroid hormone. Happily, modern research has found a way to use GH releasers to stimulate the pituitary to secrete GH. This new technology may become a major asset in any program to maintain a healthy and young body.

7. HYPOTHALAMUS

The hypothalamus could be called the granddaddy of the endocrine system even though it is not, per se, an endocrine gland. The hypothalamus could be called a neuro-endocrine organ because it controls the autonomic, or unconscious, nervous system. The activities of the hypothalamus are vital to homeostasis, the condition of inner balance within the body. It controls such bodily functions as water and temperature balance, as well as being an integrating center for biological rhythms and emotions. It exerts such powerful control over the pituitary gland that we will include it in our gland meditation so that the flow of energy is complete.

8. PINEAL GLAND

Hanging like the proverbial bat from the roof of the third ventricle, is the mysterious pineal gland that registers light through its retinic cells, from the darkness of its cave. It is also sensitive to low-intensity electromagnetic fields such as those coming from electrical equipment. The correlation between these weak fields and the increase of such diseases as cancer and leukemia in areas around them should make us all take a second look at our unwitting exposure to them.

The pineal gland is one of the two master glands of the body. Along with the pituitary, it sets the frequency of energy that is available on subtle as well as physiological levels.

The pineal gland orchestrates the body's awareness of the cyclic fluctuations in the seasons. It is wonderful to

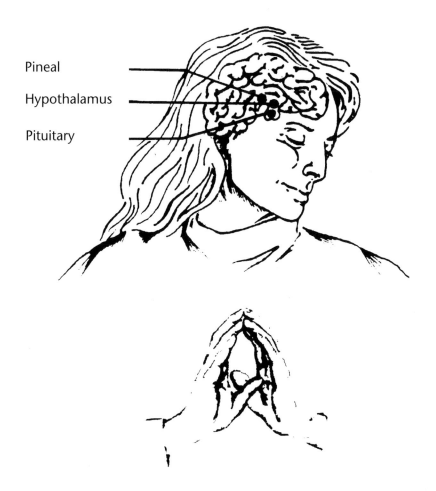

Pineal

Hypothalamus

Pituitary

79

realize that we can reap some of the benefits of our animal heritage in that we have the ability to attune to these subtle lines of information that are so important to our sense of ourselves in nature. In the future, as the weather patterns become so different, we will appreciate and hone these faculties to even higher levels.

The pineal gland, is in effect, the internal time clock that orients the body by day and night as well as what time it is in life. This is of major importance to us as we seek to re-program the body's long term time schedule so as to stop the aging process. The pineal gland is sensitive to cycles of light and darkness, and actually tells the cells of the body what time of the day and year it is. Thus, many of its functions are directly related to its sensitivity to aging. For example, the pineal gland secretes the hormone melatonin which inhibits the hypothalamus from releasing gonadotropin-releasing hormone (GNRH) that starts the maturation of the sexual glands. This protects the young from precocious and sexual adulthood until the pineal gives the signal that it is time. At puberty, there is an arc of connection between the pineal gland and the gonads that stimulates the maturity of the physical body. By the same token, as we drift towards the end of our natural life span, the secretion of melatonin drops precipitously. Here is a major clue to our participa-tion in the aging process! If we can influence the production of melatonin, we may be able to rid ourselves of an unconscious time clock. I know that we can!

Studies have shown that the administration of melato-nin to old rats not only caused them to live much longer, but the signs of old age were actually reversed and the rats became sleek and shiny coated.

In humans, melatonin seems to help fight cardiovascu-lar disease by reducing the low-density lipoproteins that clog arteries. It has also been shown to be a potentially powerful cancer inhibitor.

Melatonin is inhibited by light and is released during the night with peak secretion around 2 a.m. There is evidence that the bright lights in cities block the release of melatonin and thus it is important to protect ourselves from street lights while we sleep.

The pineal gland in its youthful state also produces other compounds that enhance life. A group of neuropep-tides called epithalamium seems to rejuvenate the body, prolong life in laboratory studies and possibly control the metabolism of glucose, leaving the animals slimmer and more energetic -- just the way you and I want to be.

While science is searching for ways to supplement production of pineal hormones, we can influence it by conscious direction, in the same way it has been proven that mental intention can slow the heart pulse, or alter the temperature of the body. We all have the power to do it.

It is the most magnificent of mysteries that the pineal gland is sensitive to light, even though it is tucked away in the absolute darkness of the brain. Way back down on the evolutionary ladder, lampreys and some lizards had pineal glands that functioned as a third eye and sensed the rhythm of the seasons by measuring the light and dark cycles. Our pineal gland still "sees" through its retinic cells and the nerves that connect it to the retina of the eye. What it sees is a part of the great mysteries of existence of life. The seeing pineal gland seems to be the point of "knowing" spoken of by the mystics. Ancient masters from many traditions around the world have spoken of the pineal gland as the "third eye," the vortex or chakra center that illuminates truth. When the third eye is opened, one is privileged to see into the depths of the soul and to witness life from the level of true mastery. Clairvoyance (clear vision), or psychic perception is the gift of the pineal. Those whose third eye is open are capable of seeing the energy fields or auras, radiating out from the chakric centers. Some people, such as myself, perceive these fields through their electric-magnetic pulsations, which are picked up by the pineal gland.

Spiritually, the pineal gland is the antennae to other dimensions. It is sensitive not only to electromagnetic fields as we recognize them, but also fields of energy which are within negative space time, faster than the speed of light. This is the realm of telepathy, intuition and the highest octave of human potential.

When the pineal gland begins to function at these levels, it usurps the blood sugar from the brain to feed the Shakti energy it is utilizing in order to function on such high levels. Shakti is the life force, divine energy that feeds the process of enlightenment. Because the Shakti requires so much energy, the blood sugar levels in the body are often imbalanced. This is why so many psychics are overweight and have blood sugar problems. Through awareness of the needs of the body on physiological as well as subtle levels, we can correct these imbalances by providing energy through our consciousness. I will show you how.

FEEDING YOUR ENDOCRINES

You can "feed" your endocrines by taking just a few moments to direct energy to them individually and as a whole. The easiest way is to send them the energy of color because the body interprets each cone of colored light as a specific frequency of energy with particular effects of which it is well aware. This makes it easy for you to influence your body in the most intricate and powerful of ways that would be very difficult if you were trying to trace or control those effects in a linear, mental fashion. The body knows how to satisfy its own interdependent aspects to function in perfection if it is given the raw material (energy) for the orchestration. The chemical and physiological geometry of the body allow simultaneous reactions to take place that can powerfully alter its dynamic state; yet all you have to do is offer your body a simple color that can trigger its energetic response. When you direct awareness and intention to an organ or place in your body and send it energy, the effect is holographic. The body can use that energy in whatever way it desires, be it physiologically or on more subtle levels, to bring itself into balance.

I recommend that you place a copy of the following chart of your endocrine system up in your bathroom or bedroom where you will see it everyday so that while you are dressing or brushing your teeth, you can simultaneously feed your endocrines by sending them the color they request for perfect, ageless health.

The process is simple: Start at the bottom of the chart, the gonads, and mentally ask them if they need to be balanced. Then go to the pancreas and continue up the chart asking each one. When you feel an intuitive call for balancing by any one of them, ask that gland what color it needs to come into balance. When you perceive the necessary color, draw it into the endocrine gland until it feels full. Then move up until all eight areas have been covered. You can finish by drawing a circle around all of them with a message to the body that they are now harmonious and functioning perfectly.

By doing this exercise, you are sending a powerful message to your body that will cause it to respond in a positive way. You are "feeding" yourself energetically and at the same time you are creating a sense of self-love, and honoring that makes the body feel vital and **ageless**. Your body is like any other being you know; it wants to feel loved and needs a minimal relationship with you in order to stay focused on life.

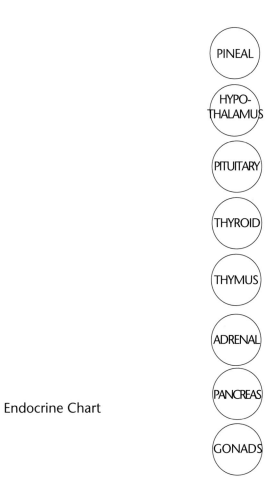

Endocrine Chart

EXERCISES FOR ETERNITY

"These exercises stimulate the chi of the internal organs by pumping the chakric energy centers and awakening the subtle energies of the endocrine glands."

In our busy modern schedule we often struggle unsuccessfully with the discipline of exercise. Although we assuage our guilt for such inactive life-styles with an occasional dash or swim, our dedication is difficult to sustain in the face of daily time pressures. Periodically we may become fanatical about some new exercise routine that we hope will totally change our shape or make us into super-beings overnight, but all this enthusiasm ultimately wanes on the downdraft of routine boredom.

The only saving grace is the view that bodies are not made to function as treadmill machines, but rather are magnificent pulsars that are cyclic in nature. This means that when you are loath to exercise, you need not make lame excuses to yourself in pretense of justification, because your body may actually be telling you not to do it at this moment! Of course, the trick is to distinguish between the rationalizations of the mind and the true voice of the body. If you simply close your eyes and ask your body, "shall I exercise today?" or, "shall I swim, run, dance or do yoga?" it will promptly reward you with a definite yes or no, according to its needs. If you ask it, however, you must defy any tendency to ignore its response; you must do what it tells you, even if you don't want to!

Time schedules can be very detrimental to body rhythms.

Perhaps you have fifteen minutes after lunch to move the body, but it may feel quite put upon to be asked to extend its energies into the muscle layers when it is happily metabolizing its food intake. You must do something to prepare it so that it can do its best for you. If you visualize the activity in which you are about to engage, for example, the body will automatically gear up for movement.

In the late afternoon the blood sugar levels tend to drop which causes irritability and a feeling of exhaustion. Chinese medicine calls this the time of the kidney. The kidney represents the deepest energy in the body and it is the kidney chi that feeds the heart. This is the time when the kidney meridian is the most active and the body may call for the assistance of blood stimulation in the form of some kind of body movement to help the filtration process. Interestingly, people often reach for the cocktail that provides instant sugar accessibility into the blood at the expense of the kidneys which must deal with the alcohol. This is the case where you feel one thing, such as tiredness, but if you asked your body, it would tell you something different. If you opted to exercise instead, the body could feel invigorated and renewed.

Years ago while I was in Bolivia, someone gave me a mimeographed copy of a little book called *The Eye of Revelation* which resurfaced in 1985 under the title of *Ancient Secret of the Fountain of Youth*. It spoke of techniques utilized by the Lamas of Tibet to maintain the body in perfect balance and health in order to facilitate their concentration on the higher realms of spirit. Though the result of these practices was that they lived extended lives without apparent aging, they did so to express the power of divine manifestation. There is a little smile that comes to me as I contemplate how people around the world might apply these techniques in order to stave the devastation of aging, and end up with a magnificent new spiritual experience of the universe and the source of life!

As I explored the text, I began to feel how the movements altered my auric field. I have always been a fairly active person physically, but I recognized immediately that this was a new octave of interaction with the body. My many pregnancies had acquainted me intimately with my internal organs from the standpoint of the stresses and strains being placed on them, but I had never had the opportunity of finding a way to replenish them for their splendid job!

The text supported my awareness of the auric field and its relationship to energy chakras in a new way. Since childhood I have experienced their presence as a force of energy radiating out of all living things, although I had never probed the essence of their source in terms of what controls the quality of those radiations. Their quality and vibrancy provided me with clues about the inner nature of a person, but I had not contemplated the long term potential of consciously stimulating these life-giving energy circuits for ourselves! I began to know the body through its parts, though it was many years and deaths later that I have come to focus on the anti-aging aspects of this knowledge. I began to dialog with my body from an internal perspective, rather than my old conversations about external presentations such as fat and weight, hair and motion. When I studied Chinese Acupuncture, I understood intrinsically how the chakras, meridians and organs commune. It was thrilling to discover a vocabulary that explains how these subtle energies feed and intertwine our internal organs.

It is my conclusion that these Tibetan exercises stimulate the chi of the internal organs by pumping the chakric energy centers and awakening the subtle energies of the endocrine glands. They are wonderful to do because you have the satisfaction of feeling that you are doing something quite physical in a condensed timeframe. This is all important to me because I become bored very quickly by repetition. The Tibetans refer to them as rites, which seems fitting since the overt action is directly related to a specific internal response. I will show them to you with a few bridging motions I feel increase their effect upon the body.

You need a space with a mat or rug on the floor to practice all the exercises in one sitting. All of them can be done alone, and some are well-suited for quick energy boosts in the office or on the run.

RITE 1

The first rite is the practice of spinning which I have mentioned in all my other books because of its effect upon the Emotional Body. As one spins clockwise, negative residues are literally flung out of the body as the energies take up the expansion pattern. This is a wonderful exercise because it strengthens the bridge between left and right hemispheres and thus helps us become more holographic. The chakras are greatly increased by this action because they are essentially energies within spinning vortexes. As the vortex is increased, the life force becomes stronger and more directed.

All you have to do is begin spinning with your arms held out to the sides. Follow your right arm so that you spin around to your right. You can use the dancer's technique of "spotting" whereby you fix your attention on something in front of you at eye level as you turn. This lessens the feeling of imbalance and allows you to spin longer before you feel dizzy. The ancients practiced the spinning for twenty-one full turns, but don't feel discouraged if you feel dizzy after half that many. It is like anything else in that you must help the body adjust to the new motion and then increase slowly as your body gains mastery over it. Do **stop** as soon as you feel slightly dizzy. Lay down on the floor and breathe deeply before you begin the next rite. Raise your hands above your head to stretch your back.

RITE TWO

This rite appears similar to typical abdominal exercises. By raising the head to the chest, you are creating an extra stimulus to the solar plexus chakra and the conception vessel moving through the center of the trunk. Be sure you have a thick rug to protect your back as you lay on the floor. Place your hands on the floor at your sides, palms down with your fingers close together. Taking an in-breath, raise your head and your legs simultaneously towards each other. Tuck your chin to your chest as you bring your legs up vertically towards your head. It is important to maintain the knees in the locked position. Now, slowly lower the legs while exhaling your breath and relaxing your head back on the floor. Relax all the muscles and repeat the rite as many times as you can without strain. The optimal number is twenty-one times. You can do half that number twice a day and see amazing results.

91

Rite 2

Rite two extension

Upon sitting up, stretch your legs out in front of you. Starting at the thigh area, stroke down the outside of your legs with your hands until you reach your feet. Grab your feet on the outside, pulling your head as close to your straight knees as possible. This is not an easy exercise. I often find myself groaning as I do it, but the promise of straight legs, rather than the saddle-bags of lowered hormonal action and digestive sluggishness, spurs me on.

Rite two extension

RITE THREE

I love this next motion as it is so powerful for opening the solar plexus and the heart. As we begin life drawing in through the umbilical area, we tend to continue that habit of sucking in to the solar plexus, which is the seat of the Emotional Body, without any awareness of what we are taking in. All kinds of emotional energies enter in this way. Psychically, we attract negative emotions that relate to those we ourselves are carrying. Thus, the fear or anger inside of us acts as a magnet to people who are carrying the same kind of energies. While in the midst of a crowd, we draw those energies into us without ever even knowing it, though we may comment how shopping malls and theaters make us "tired." Contraction interferes with the functioning of the solar plexus ganglion that relays messages to the brain relevant to our sense of safety. The "fight or flight" reflex is stimulated by emotional reaction every bit as much as by physical response. This rite provides an extension and a powerful lifting of the entire trunk, which is the opposite of a defensive, contractive stance. By doing this motion, you are reversing the energy flow and raising the energy up to the heart area. As you do the motion, it feels almost as if the heart is reaching up to happiness, and indeed, it makes you feel happy to do it.

Kneel down with your toes curled forward so that the bottoms touch the floor. Place your hands behind you to hold the back of your legs under the buttocks. Exhale as you lower your head and neck to touch your chin to your chest. Now, breathe in and bring your head back while arching your back fully. Lean back as far as you can and keep your eyes gently closed so that your focus is inward while you experience the freedom of your extended body. Come back to the original straight position and begin again.

extension

When you are through with this series of motions, extend your arms at shoulder level straight out in front of you and lean back without arching your back. You will feel this stretching the *facia lata* at the outer thighs. This area reflexes to the intestines and is wonderful for balancing their job of elimination.

98

Rite three

RITE FOUR

This next rite seems equally difficult at first, but sixty and seventy-year olds can do it. It actually causes a pleasant stimulation throughout the sacral area which stirs the reflexes, meridians, and thus the energies going to and from the sexual area of the body and down the legs.

Sit with your back straight and your legs out in front of you. Place your arms straight down at your sides with palms on the floor. Breathe out as you touch your chin to your chest, and then gathering your strength with your inhaling breath, raise your head all the way back as you lift your body up horizontal to the floor by pushing onto your feet with your arms supporting you. You will now be making a table with your body and it is good to tense all your muscles before you sweep back down feeling your buttocks brushing the floor and returning to the sitting position. Continue the same deep breathing between movements and begin again.

Rite 4

RITE FIVE

This is my favorite rite as it brings an immediate change in the energy currents of the body. It makes one feel strong and invigorated and brings a happy glow to the face. I feel that it is one of the most powerful in terms of speeding up the chakric vortexes.

Start as if you were going to do push-ups with your body, face down on the floor. Both the arms and legs are held straight supporting you and are spread out about the width of your shoulders and hips. Begin by extending the head back and arching the back so that the body is in a sagging position. Now breathe in and bend at the hips making your body into a living pyramid with your sacrum at the apex. Tuck your chin to chest and tighten all your muscles for a moment before you swing down with an exhalation into the half moon with your head backward, holding your muscles tight for a moment again.

After these five rites, there is a sixth rite which is the most powerful of all. I will discuss it in the sequence I place it for the full series of exercises. However, if you are in a hurry and are ready for this kind of energetic frequency in your body, you can perform it at this point, using the five Tibetan rites as a complete unit.

Rite 5

While in a cross-legged position you can do a simple spine stretch that facilitates the energy throughout the spinal column and increases the flexibility of your neck.

Place your palms down on your knees and slowly turn your head to gaze over one shoulder. As you do, you will feel the pleasant stretching and twisting of your spine. Repeat in the other direction and continue several times breathing in as you turn your neck and head over the shoulder and exhale while returning to the center. You can create an even rhythm with your breathing and movement. This Taoist exercise will bring you into a deep state of relaxation and will facilitate meditation.

Now I'll show you a Taoist exercise that strengthens the digestion and brings balance and harmony to the body while increasing vitality:

Sit cross-legged and straight-backed as comfortably as you can and place your hands towards the knees with the fists clenched and palms facing up. This keeps the energy circulating in the body, rather than dispersing it. Run your tongue from the left corner of your mouth, across the gums and up around the roof to draw a path in a circle. This is a counter-clockwise motion. The Taoists say you should do it thirty-six times to activate the flow of saliva and then swish it forewords and backwards with your tongue another thirty-six times until your mouth is quite full of saliva. Now you will swallow it in three parts which represent heaven, earth and man to the Taoists. It should be a vigorous swallow with the intent to send it down into the abdomen. Listen for the sound of the saliva in the belly! Repeat two to three times.

THE TURTLE

This is one of the most comprehensive exercises I can teach you to influence the **Ageless Body**. The Taoists call it the turtle exercise because it emulates the movements of a turtle stretching out its head. It stimulates all the nerves bringing energy in and out of the brain while relaxing and opening the neck area. The neck is of vital importance to us because it is the passageway of the central nervous system and thus the key to our entire body. All the yang meridians converge at the base of the neck behind the head which makes it a powerful place of protection to the body. Esoterically, the neck is the place where we hold our will and thus, if we can make the neck more fluid and flexible, we can change the rigid perspectives that cause us so much difficulty and separation in life.

The throat is our crucial communication center both verbally as well as physically since the thyroid and parathyroid glands which control so much of the body's metabolism are located here. The turtle exercise opens the throat area completely and stretches the entire spine while strengthening and dissolving tiredness and stiffness of the neck and shoulder muscles. It is important to do this exercise slowly in the rhythm you imagine a turtle would use.

The breathing pattern is reverse so that you will inhale as you touch your chin to your chest. You can feel the stretch on the back of your neck and your shoulders will relax downward.

Now, bring your shoulders up toward your ears like a turtle pulling back into its shell while you begin to exhale slowly as you drop your head back to rest on the back of your neck. Repeat at least twelve times.

The turtle should be practiced in concert with two other motions which greatly influence the endocrine glands and the chakras.

First, as you lift your neck in exhalation, squeeze your anal sphincter as if stopping the flow of urine. This is the action of the all-important pubococcygeal muscles that strengthen the pelvic floor and are used in love-making. Both men and women can control these muscles drawing the energy up from the genital area to nourish the sexual organs and thus the entire body. Hold the pubococcygeal muscle tight until you again bring the chin down during inhalation. Relax them while you inhale. As you become proficient at combining these internal and external motions, you can hold the pubococcygeal muscle through one or two whole cycles.

The second motion is the rubbing of the breasts for women and the lower abdomen for men, in unison with the rest of the exercise. This seems very complicated at first and demands some effort to master. However, it has such a profound effect on the body that it is well worth it!

If you are a man, place both your hands fingers downward, over your lower abdomen just above the pubic bone. As you execute the turtle, rub both hands in a clockwise motion from the pubic bone to the right, up to the belly button, and down your left side back to the pubis. Do this until you feel heat in the lower abdominal area.

If you are a female, place your hands with the fingers facing down towards the pelvic bone, between your breasts. There are two directions to rub depending on the needs of the body.

Starting with the fingers between the nipples, rub up and outward to each side of the breasts, down around and up through to the starting position, having traced all the way around the breast. Do this about three times as fast as you do the rest of the turtle moves, or about thirty-six times to the twelve motions of the turtle.

Once you have arrived at perfect hormonal and physical balance, you will no longer need to do the rubbing part of the exercise. Do **not** do this exercise during menstruation because at that time you will be wanting the energy to flow out of the body, not up. It is very common for women who practice this exercise daily to stop menstruating. This fact should give you a clue about how powerful these internal exercises are in terms of regulating the flows of bodily energies.

By doing the turtle exercise, you are giving a strong mandate to your body not to engage in reproductive activities!

After completing the Turtle, your body will be relaxed and balanced. This is a good point for meditation, as your focus and consciousness will be deep within.

Turtle

RITE SIX

The Tibetans say that this sixth rite will make you into a super-being, but that it is only for those who have chosen to be celibate. I have taught it to hundreds of people and it is a standard exercise for the students of my Nizhoni School for Global Consciousness where we are focusing our energies on different octaves. Let me definitely warn you that it will change the quality of your love-making and I would recommend it only for people who have become aware of tantric sexuality or have had experiences of sexual merging such as the sensation of becoming both partners; the male and the female. If the focus of your love-making is climatic release and you have not learned to draw the energy back into your body, just skip this rite. If you use sex as a release, this exercise is not appropriate for you as it brings the energy too far up in the body. It will not only make you feel very uncomfortable, it will have a diminishing effect on your sexual urge and expression. This is not for people who identify themselves with sexual expression.

What you are doing is **transmuting the reproductive energy!** Therefore, this rite is absolutely contra-indicated for pregnant women or couples who are at this moment wishing to have children. There are no studies of its effect on the reproductive cycles; perhaps one day it will be used as a birth control measure with enlightenment side-effects!

Fulfilling sexual expression is one of the gifts of embodiment and should never be suppressed or restricted because we think it is outside the spiritual realm. Just look at the sad struggle some of the religiously ordained have had with this concept. It is the most sacred energy we possess, we simply have never understood all of its ramifications on energetic levels. Transmuting if from procreative energies to higher vibratory frequencies is equally the choice and opportunity of each individual.

However, this sixth rite will cause you to become much more sensitive to the sexual currents within your body and it will facilitate their motion up through the higher chakras so that they are available to you as creative energy, mental acuity, intuitive and healing forces!

Stand comfortably and exhale as you bend from the waist, placing your hands on your knees. Expel the last bit of air from your lungs and without taking in a new breath, return to an erect position. Place your hands with fingers to the front on your hips and press down as hard as you can.

118

This will raise your shoulders and chest up, and it is important to suck in your abdomen at the same time. After I hold in my abdomen, I also squeeze the pubococcygeal muscle up to emphasize the upward thrust.

Hold this position and bring your closed eyeballs to the point between the eyebrows so that all this lower chakric energy will rise up to the highest centers. When you must take a breath, breathe in through your nose and then exhale through the mouth as you drop your arms down to your sides to relax. Take in several normal breaths through the nose and mouth before beginning again. At least three repetitions are necessary for most people to feel the sexual energy lifting upward.

If you look at yourself in the mirror after doing this exercise, you will be shocked at the shiny look in your eyes and how absolutely radiant you appear. This is true beauty! You will also feel a steady kind of clarity that helps you to exude a new level of confidence for, indeed, you will be a new person capable of higher and more conscious aware-ness. This is true beauty. It is the kiss of eternity bestowed on those who can experience themselves within the embrace of the **Ageless Body.**

Rite 6

SEXUALITY AND THE AGELESS BODY

*"If you will lift your sexual energy up into your heart, you will begin to feel the giggle of your **Ageless Body**."*

Sexual energy is instrumental to the **Ageless Body.** It is by virtue of the hormones and their master glands connected to sexual function that the body stays in a perpetual state of "juicy" youth. While the physical body has its primordial agenda, ever nudging us towards procreation, we may have our own response to the magnificent currents with which it titillates and entices us. That same orgasmic rush that flushes precious energy from the body can be orchestrated and turned upward to vitalize our entire being. It can also be transformed into creative feats and great powers of knowing or healing.

Through conscious application, the body's life-enhancing secretions and substances can serve our needs in many ways. The sexual-physical body can be transformed into a higher octave energy body that nourishes the entire multi-dimensional Being. The sexual energy can be awakened from its base in the genitals, fed by the endocrine glands and released throughout the entire body to create an infinite helix of **ageless** energy.

Since sexual energy is a "raw" energy, it can be focused on almost any level. For example, if a person suffers from fatigue, mental confusion or even chronic sore throats, the sexual energy is powerful enough to strengthen the immune system via increased self-identification. It is really the handmaiden of the divine soul because it is the vehicle that transports soul into body.

Sexual energy is directly linked to the force of creativity, though it often plays the adversary and tries to restrict the creative surge by entrapping it in the lower octaves. Because it is coupled with biological sensations, it will tend to focus its force within the body without extending to more subtle forms of expression.

I remember very clearly how I suffered from the connection between the two. Especially as a teenager, whenever I would get a strong creative impulse, whether it was to make something or even to write, my sexual currents would immediately become activated as well. Often I simply could not withstand the intensity and would dissipate the energy by dancing or running or doing anything I could to free myself of its electrifying charge. It took me years to learn to contain the frequencies and push the sexual urge through the channels of creative expression. I am sure this is the reason young people so often start and abandon their creative projects; great beginnings are left half finished because the young person cannot hold the high energy voltage.

This aspect of sexual energy that wants to be released is the cause of much sexual dissatisfaction and misunderstanding between women and men, who both make love, all too often, for the release of tension, rather than to heighten communion. It is the most commonly expressed disappointment by women, who then say that the best part of sex for them is the closeness they seek after the act. They seem to feel that the act itself is mostly focused on the needs of the man. On the other hand, men feel judged and truly uncertain of how to make love to women outside of their own rushing pulse. Men often come to closure of sexual energy when women are just beginning to move towards it. The yang rhythm is basically a linear crescendo, while the yin tends towards a rolling, rising and falling pulse. A lot of this out-of-sync rhythm can be dissolved if the man will focus on foreplay that allows the woman to have some of her experiences first; then the couple can join each other at a closer pitch.

A very rewarding interplay is the conscious bringing together of the energies that can be accomplished by tantric and other techniques, such as the breathing exercises I give in the book *Feminine Fusion*. By sending and receiving breath between the partners, a powerful charge of energy is built up that dissolves the blocks to profound union and heightens the body's sensual experience of touch. As this happens, a much more profound awareness of energy exchange on subtle levels occurs, and one would never return to the old ways of intercourse.

Climax is the closure of the sexual act in terms of the rush of energy which exits the body; however, it also opens the space for the next wave which is a more subtle, but equally powerful, energy. After climax the body must rebalance itself from the exertion and loss. Here is a point where both partners can draw the energy from the genital area back up through the endocrine system. This revitalizes the gonads and feeds the body's meridians and chakras, which have been opened emotionally as well as energetically from the exchange of energy passing through the joined auric fields. If you do this together while still in the embrace of love, the effect is a beautiful affirmation of your respect and caring for your own bodies, enhancing your capacity to merge in new ways. Sharing the juices by uniting into one body, and then utilizing the energy that has been exchanged, can bring a couple into a very deep level of energetic communion.

Because the result of a strong gonadal system is vibrant health for the whole body, you must preserve its vitality even if it will not be involved in procreative functions. It is important to teach the body to transcend its purely reproductive functionings and apply the energy that may origi-nate in the lower chakras to recharge the rest of the body.

If you seek an **Ageless Body**, you must become aware of your energy stores and be able to notice when these vital energies have drained from you. You can learn to draw the fluidic spark back up into you during and after making love so that your whole being can ride these most powerful currents of life.

CELIBACY AND THE AGELESS BODY

Most spiritual groups who understand the ancient knowledge of the body do not recommend that one waste precious life force in sexual activity, because without the disciplined and enlightened (tantric) practice of energy flow, the body will indeed lose its power.

In fact, the value or detriment of sexual expression in relation to spiritual laws have been hotly debated through the centuries. Celibacy has been a mandatory contract for many religious leaders and teachers throughout the centu-ries because of the belief that the only marriage possible is one with God. The power of sexual energy to pervade thoughts and sway actions has always been recognized as well as feared. Religious hierarchies have never had any patience with split loyalty, and a man who might whisper to his wife simply could not be tolerated.

The possibility of the divine entering into flesh has always been rejected, thus leaving sexuality sentenced to reside only in the lower chakras, devoid of any honor or grace. Many religious groups believe that you cannot know God until you turn your attention away from all aspects of "worldly" reality. However, the power of sexuality over human lives remains undaunted by the proclamations of religious orders and self-styled purists.

In today's world, celibacy is an impractical alternative for most seekers. The monastic path of the solitary cave is no longer a viable choice in a world that cries for participation. (Living alone is considered "abnormal," and few can conceive of relationships that are not built on the basis of mutual sexual exchanges.) Yet, the communion of the soul could profoundly alter the expression of love and sharing. This would not necessarily exclude sexual behavior, but would change the way it is carried out.

Perhaps another perspective would be to allow the divine to inhabit the world with you. What if you could somehow bestow a higher frequency to your sexual-physical body so that it could be aligned with a new order of spiritual expression? This, I predict, will be the direction of the future. As fulfillment in the body will be less and less to procreate or release pent up energy, other creative expressions will naturally begin to unfold. To shut off the sexual current leads only in the direction of death, because ultimately the body cannot live without its life force energy. You don't, however, need to express it only through the genitals. You can "massage" your glands so they can flush their precious life sparks into your body to keep it powerful and lively. The juices that open the body must not be allowed to dry up, but rather they must be joined with the gonads and then lifted back up to nourish your potential **ageless body**.

Once that upward current has been achieved, it is almost unbearable to express it singularly in the lower chakric frequencies. For those of us who have left that level behind, it would be physically painful to try to use these energies in this way because the electric-fluidic currents have established an upward direction. The freedom and increase of energy available when the sexual force is transcended is far greater that a few minutes of genital stimulation, because the universal orgasmic force cannot be matched by purely sexual standards. The power of this energy as it transcends the human sexual repertoire and moves up through the chakric systems to participate within the higher realms of consciousness is almost unlimited. The Five Tibetan Rites referred to it as a "super-human" level of existence. Its effect on awareness and energy for healing and creativity is boundless.

Thus, the whole concept of celibacy needs a new, more viable framework. Perhaps there will even evolve other words and vocabularies to express such a multi-dimensional, cosmic view of the sexual-physical body in its divine embrace with the spiritual body.

THE WANING OF THE CHI

After the age of thirty-five, men and women need to become aware of sexual currents as a precious source of bodily energy that must be carefully monitored. The force of kidney energy which feeds the heart begins to wane, so that a wise person must learn to replenish and retrieve their energy after the sexual act. "Holding the seed" is widely recommended as a practice that allows the intimacy of relationship without losing the delicate energy that can help open the body to enlightenment and, at the very least, awaken the Light Body.

Mother Nature, as if to place one last fertile seed, gives women their sexual prime at this time (thirty-six to forty years) so that they will feel the strong desires of the body and open to the forces of nature. Here is one of those Cosmic Jokes wherein the man begins to think of guarding his strength and the woman begins a concerted effort to lure his seed, not because she consciously thinks about procreation, but for the intense pleasure she has discovered in her body.

The pleasure from sexual experience does not necessarily decrease for men as time goes by, but the use of it can be more conscious and appreciated, rather than recklessly wasted. The old Chinese texts on sexuality astutely pointed out that here was a case for combining older women and younger men since they are both within the awakening of sexual-physical expression. Likewise, the older man and younger woman also have a symbiotic match; she is good for his image of himself and his sense of virility, though wasting his seed is definitely not recommended. The mature man knows how to wait for his younger lover and has learned the wisdom of riding her sexual currents.

If you are approaching the menopausal era of your life, or are a man past the age of thirty-five years, it is crucial for you to access your sexual energy on more than just the genital levels. You will want to preserve and awaken it to serve your whole body. If you do the endocrine exercises and the Exercises for Eternity, you will be able to keep your physical body young, radiant and full of life. Since sexual energy is the creative force of the universe, you can extend it to rejuvenate yourself and heal others, as well as to open creative channels you never dreamed existed.

The awareness of higher consciousness is often just awakening as the procreative stage of physical function is ending. Indubitably, this is a plan set in motion by an all-knowing intelligence of the evolutionary process. At this more highly developed stage, you can begin to wield your life with the knowing intention of one who can command the body, regardless of its impulsive urges. With this mastery comes great pleasure, as the body is capable of rewarding you with a much higher affinity to subtle nuances.

You are so much more than your mere physicality, yet it forms the base from which you can learn to soar into higher realms of universal function. As you apply your sexual energy to fuel your physical body, you begin to see how it affects your emotional and spiritual bodies as well. There can be no doubt that sexuality greatly influences how you experience yourself emotionally.

SEXUALITY: THE EMOTIONAL TRIGGER

We will always desire to touch and be touched by another as long as the veil of separation from our true source remains a part of human experience. Indeed, the sensuality of the body is one of the many gifts given to us to support and encourage the experience of embodiment.

Sexuality is a great test for the Emotional Body because it triggers all of the deep feelings we carry about ourselves. Until puberty the sexual connection to our sense of self is vague because it is not a part of how we address the world outside us. Once past puberty, the biological pull of procreation brings into play the presentation of the body as the major lure to gain a mate, and thus to procreate. This is painful for most of us as we begin to measure our self-worth on a scale of physical attributes. The temptation to wield our body as an enticement to the world becomes almost irresistible, but at the same time, as we compare ourselves with others, we begin to feel insecure about our value. Up until this point in life, we might have attained a goal through sheer drive or effort, but now there seems to be nothing outside of some mystical attraction mechanism that does not yield to trying or any other discipline we might have learned to bring us what or who we want.

The process of sexual maturation is an incredible vortex of energy that sucks you in and then thrusts you out into a frightening and competitive world where you tend to use your sexuality as a sword of emotional defense, even after you have found your partners and should be settling down to a "comfortable" life. As long as you view yourself through the marketplace of desirability in terms of the physical body, you will remain in a prison of anxiety and insecurity. Perhaps this is why you tend to use sexual energy as an emotional weapon, rather than the divine gift of loving that it truly is.

The blissful feelings of closeness with another are there to enhance profound communion, rather than as a cloak in which to hide. However, in love relations it is difficult to separate the closeness you seek from the dependency it instills in you *vis a vis* your partners. You project onto them the power to make you happy and then feel utterly helpless to find a sense of fulfillment without them. You are especially dependent on them for sexual pleasure. This is a very inflammable situation because the performance of lovemaking becomes so identified with the message of being loved, or not.

Many of the fights between sexual partners stem from harboring feelings about what happens or does not happen during sexual expression. You can free yourself from this web of emotion by realizing that **you** are entirely responsible for the sensations that you have in your body.

Begin by asking yourself if you are willing to be present in your body, and then ask your body if it can feel your presence! The gift of sensuality can be focused in any direction. For example, caressing a rose could be totally orgasmic if you are willing to allow enough tactile involvement, by rubbing its velvety texture, to carry you away.

If you seek spectacular sexual fulfillment, you must come to know your own body in intimate detail so that when your partner touches you, you can **use** that touch to carry the stimulation as far as it can go, which depends completely on your capacity to focus on the sensation and amplify it.

If you have forgotten who you are, you will not recognize your own timeless bodies and **ageless** emotions. You may have not yet discovered your own blissful sensuality and still be hoping someone will show it to you. The truth is that your connection to the spark of life comes from inside you and it is **ageless**. It is not dependent on your emotional ties with the outside world, but rather on your relationship with your own body.

You can learn to experience sexual energy as pure

energy in and of itself, which will lead you to what I called "Cosmic Orgasm," as described in my book *Ecstasy is a New Frequency*. These are the higher realms of sexual experience that happen throughout the entire body, rather than just the genitals, as it aligns to new frequencies. People everywhere are beginning to experience these rare octaves of sexual potential and this will set in motion a new kind of sexuality that is not based on what you can extract from a partner, but rather the intensity of energy available to you, with or without a partner!

If you can learn to move deeply within your body, you can use it as a finely tuned instrument of loving expression that you share with your partner, rather than passively waiting for the other to bring the energy to you.

SEXUALITY AND THE SPIRITUAL BODY

Though it seems that the sexual component of spiritual understanding is often the last aspect to lift into the light, many people are discovering how to express their deep love for others without holding it in the confinement of sexuality. You may feel a mysterious closeness or attraction for someone you meet, only to discover too late that it really has nothing to do with sexual bonding, but rather is a result of kindred souls who have traveled the eons together. It is sometimes hard to distinguish between a strong sexual feeling and a familiarity that seems both old and new. Once you can discern between the two and have learned to view each relationship in karmic terms, you will be free to explore a kind of intimacy that few humans have shared.

It is fascinating for me to observe this soul phenomenon during group workshops at The Light Institute. Perfect strangers come together from around the world and feel a recognition of each other that they would ordinarily identify as a sexual spark. Their Higher Selves teach them to move into profound and intimate relationship, and what might have been wasted on a brief sexual encounter becomes a loving soul bond that supports and encourages the spiritual path of each one. They leave their six-day spiritual quest feeling very much renewed and alive, with a revelation of the fulfillment bestowed on them by their Spiritual Body.

Sexual energy is truly a sacred energy. It brought you into life through your soul connection to your parents who gifted you a physical vehicle with which to absorb and transcend your soul lessons. Through sexual energy you can move in exquisite concert with another being and together create new life! This mysterious feat has become devalued in an overpopulated world, but with the scourge of AIDS, it will be seen differently by future generations who will view new life as a sacred and conscious act.

The enactment of sexual surging opens the auric field to allow you to embrace the nuances of another's thoughts, feelings and bodily states. If you become aware of this intertwining, you can caress and comfort on levels that have never been reached in human relationship. All healing is spiritual at its core, and to give in these ways will always be part of the purpose of embodiment.

If you tap your divine sexual energy at the higher frequencies, your whole life begins to transcend. Relationships will necessarily go through change as your deepened sexual experience carries you to a new depth of human fusion. From there the communication and sharing become transformed so that the "soul-touching" echoes out into all other aspects of your life.

As your conception brought you into body, the threshold back across the veil becomes available to you when that same current courses upward again in search of its origin. The sexual current longs to reproduce the divine source from whence it came so as to not live alone within the limitation of the third-dimensional world. Just as the sexual-physical body hungers to recreate itself by moving one step on to the next generation of itself, the sexual-spiritual body enacts the fusion of life through its marriage in the sea of the cosmos.

Do not be afraid to open your heart to the force of your spiritual nature as it awakens a new kind of sexual pulse. Human sexuality is ripe for a dramatic leap of expression. Each being makes love with a deep hope of touching something so profound that the ego is relinquished and the Higher Self encompasses the whole of conscious experience. Ultimately, to "have sex" using only the genitals is an empty, flat and one-dimensional exercise of isolation. It will not continue as a part of human expression because there is something stirring that is seeking an alignment of heart and soul. If you will lift your sexual energy up into your heart, you will begin to feel the giggle of your **ageless body**.

THE AGELESS HEART

"We must learn to perceive our heart as a faithful and loyal employee who, in the face of clearly expressed direction or command, will always follow the mandate given by the master of the body, which is our consciousness."

The heart is the focal point for the highest octave of human expression; it is the citadel of unconditional love and human compassion. Like the proverbial evolutionary tree, the heart is the only passageway through which humanity will progress up to new octaves of blissful experience and frequencies of consciousness that will allow it to fulfill the mandate of human potential.

The passage necessitates our comprehension of the delicate interplay between our physical selves and our emotional and spiritual selves. Nowhere is that symbiotic relationship more evident than in the functioning of the human heart. Faithfully beating throughout our lives, our heart keeps the body alive while simultaneously tuning the energies of our emotional and spiritual faculties so that the lessons we learn can open us up to the heart's powerful potential as the vehicle for all transcendence. We must experience the heart holographically, and as we strengthen this magnificent muscle physically, we can expand it emotionally and spiritually in order to have a truly healthy heart and life.

This is the planet of the heart chakra, which means that all of us are here to learn about the heart's potential to lift our spirits up to octaves of profound human emotion and compassion. Through the vehicle of the human heart, we can express feelings that transform the experience of life. It is the greatest of human lessons, designed to teach us all how to express and commune through the heart. As each disease tells us something specific about the theme of the lessons we are learning, the heart teaches us about relationship as a channel of self-expression. Even our magnificent circulatory system is symbolic of the thousand pathways for give and take that exchange the life force energy between so many different levels of cellular and organ communities.

Because of the importance of our heart themes, there is a direct correlation between our expression of relationship one to another, and the health of the heart. Every heart seeks love and communion because these are the energies that provide the force of human transcendence and evolution. Deep within us we know that our desire for relationship is more than our immediate feelings, but it is something that touches the core of our existence. When we feel that we are failing on emotional levels, our whole sense of purpose undergoes a profound shift towards despair. It is the despair and emptiness that contributes heavily to heart trouble. Medical doctors should always delve into the emotional relationships of their patients to reveal this sensitive correlation.

It is even worse for those who have learned not to express any emotional feelings or dependence. One cannot help but think of the hard-driving executive who sits at the top of the pile, alone and all too often holding the compensatory bag of money and power, but who rarely has the luxury of sharing his or her deepest emotions; here waits a prime target for heart disease. Rarely has a person ever suffered heart trouble of any kind when there has not been some precipitous undercurrent of separation or emotional stress.

The heart provides the pumping mechanism that moves the energy of life through the body. While the heart muscle incessantly pumps and distributes the blood through our bodies, it is nevertheless influenced by our emotional presence and our will to live. Though the heart is a muscle, a mechanically designed apparatus of the body, it is acutely attuned and influenced by emotion and by stress.

All stress inevitably is sourced in the fear that the sense of the self, in accordance to judgement from the outside world, will not be successful. We worry about our jobs and our future, we worry that we may not find or continue relationship, and all these things reflect our profound inner anxiety because we do not know who we are or the true purpose of our lives. Without this essential knowledge, self-love seems unattainable and we are cast upon the sea of

interminable struggle.

The heart is symbolic of our deepest, most profound connections to life. Every relationship we have is activated or tempered by the heart. Even those distant business or competitive relationships are shaped by the availability of heart energy where trust and admiration influence the potential of the relationship.

If the heart is closed, we miss the freshness of life that renews and pushes us onward. The beauty of the world seems meaningful only if we feel connected to and successful in our relationships. The heart narrows its access to love through faulty conclusions on the part of the Emotional Body that preclude any new experience of love because of its clinging to the painful past. In a traumatic situation, when we feel the fear that love will be taken away, the heart is activated by the emotional shock and will beat furiously and then constrict itself in an effort to shut out the pain.

On the other side of the equation, when we feel love, there is a breakthrough of this energy which lifts up into the heart. Emotional energy rising up into the heart region creates a fantastic sense of expansion and lightness in the chest. This is a physiological orchestration as well as an emotional one because the release of constriction on the solar plexus ganglion opens the flow of energy upward through the heart. The heart is not only the poetic expression of love, but much of the actual experience of love is felt through the heart. It may pound or change its beat when we feel love. We might feel great warmth or the tickle of a feather in the heart as we are touched by a loving gesture.

Below the level of the heart, the energies of the Emotional Body contain a consciousness imprinted mostly by the ego's eternal quest for survival and self-gratification. When the consciousness is locked within the solar plexus, Emotional Body octave, there is a strangulation of the energy in the heart.

BIOFEEDBACK FROM THE HEART

Because the heart is anchored into all our realms of consciousness, it is a veritable biofeedback machine that constantly keeps the score of life's game. All the successes and failures in the arenas of mind, body and emotion are tallied upon the scoreboard of the heart which then continuously attempts to compensate for the imbalances and the stresses. If you recognize that the **Ageless Body** is fueled by a peaceful will to live, you can use this biofeedback from the heart as an amplification of your joy at just being alive in body.

After my last death experience with the involvement of the left ventricle, my heart became an instantaneous biofeedback recording through which any tenseness would be exposed by a physical feeling of heaviness in the heart. I've discovered that the sensation is actually caused by a "squeezing" in which any anger or negativity literally blocks the flow of energy so that the heart tenses and squeezes itself. I found that if I did not let go immediately of whatever it was that I was holding, the tightness would turn into lasting chest pain, a clear reminder that no daily occurrence or momentary overreaction was worth my life.

It was the most graphic demonstration of how the heart muscle itself responds to negativity and how negativity cuts us off from life. It is very sobering to witness the abuse of the body, even through our temporal or superficial emotions. This has taught me, sometimes very painfully, that frustration and annoyance are not worth the responses they produce in the body. Although I have often wished that this particular biofeedback heart reflex would not occur, it has forced me to re-evaluate my perception and my response to daily stress. When some negativity occurs, I immediately take a deep breath and command my heart to open. This prevents any squeezing and gives me the physiological sensation that I am "big" enough to overcome the obstacle.

I have learned to desensitize my reaction to external stress, for the message in the body is direct, " It is not worth this!"

It is important to redirect the energy that has built up. I do this by sending color to the situation or person. The energy is pushing to get out so I simply exchange the negative energy for a rebalancing force. I ask internally, "What color do you need to come into balance and be released?" Then I focus on sending the color that I psychically perceive is being asked for. This technique makes it so much easier to let go because you are taking action, which is always what the Emotional Body is demanding. But at the same time you are teaching your Emotional Body to respond without defensiveness or self-justification and instead move towards resolution and freedom.

It is a most magnificent feeling to witness yourself being able to master the process of releasing stress through simply changing your mind as to the energy you are willing to give any situation. You can command the Emotional Body with your consciousness to let go by simply directing its focus away from the self and towards the source of the stress with a positive energy.

This is really a process of surrender. Perhaps one of the most important lessons for the ego is to recognize that surrender is not the loss of the self, but an opportunity to expand and include new energies. Surrender is always the process of opening to a higher expression of the self and its wisdom; it is to the Higher Self only that we truly surrender ourselves. This kind of surrendering allows us a more holographic perspective of how and why things happen the way they do. Our Higher Self may use all these situations and relationships to teach us the lessons that will ultimately set us free from emotional and mental anguish.

FEAR IN THE HEART

Though cancer is fast overtaking heart disease as the major body killer, fear of heart trouble is still of foremost concern to many people. Heart disease is such a major killer that throughout the world there is a collective fear pertaining to the heart. Whole families live with the shadow of any inherited tendency towards heart problems. Once someone is diagnosed with any kind of heart disease, they, as well as their family, live in constant terror that this overpowering force will strike them and render them helpless or bring death. The very fear of the possibility increases its probability because the heart is a conscious entity who is perpetually listening to our thoughts and feelings and is following our tendencies. Focus your attention on something that really frightens you and feel how your heart will change its rhythm in response!

Fear of the heart is a great health hazard. When people have palpitations, arrhythmic disorders or pain, they freeze up in fear and wait to see what will happen to them, as if this were an assault by an enemy over whom they have no control.

In Chinese medicine the kidney meridian is said to hold our deepest ancestral chi, or energy. The kidney chi nourishes the heart but residual fear puts undue stress on the adrenal glands that must respond to "fight or flight" situations. They become overreactive and burden the heart. The concept that we receive certain inherited energy from our forefathers is very interesting because we also receive from them the imprints of the experiences they had as they lived and died. Life in the past was very hard and filled with stress. The memories of our distant parents and their primordial fears must be erased. It is imperative that we clear our genetic reservoir of the fear and strife they accumulated so that we do not pass such aging factors on to our children.

Having grown up in a household of heart disease, I was certainly programmed to fear my heart. Many of us have a pre-programmed relationship of fear in which we wrongly perceive that the heart is some powerful and distant authority that runs our body without any possible recourse or choice of our own. Our silent assumption that our heart is going to fail us or strike us, puts us on course for just such a possibility. Even the word "heart attack" carries with it an ominous expression of our fear that the heart will turn on us at some unexpected moment when the truth is exactly the opposite.

So much good could be done to alleviate heart disease through teaching us to recognize our own powerful influence over our hearts. We must learn to perceive our heart as a faithful and loyal employee who, in the face of clearly expressed direction or command, will always follow the mandate given by the master of the body, which is our consciousness. Our hearts will perform their task if we will but give them the few essential nourishing elements they require and turn our unquenchable thirst for love into a nourishing flow of appreciation and tenderness towards our own heart.

REGIMEN FOR THE AGELESS HEART

You can focus your heart for health and joy. There are many things you can do to support and strengthen it. It is time to recognize that you are the master and the healer of your own body. Do not be afraid to work on yourself; your heart is waiting for you to work with it. I'd like to share with you the processes I do for my heart.

TALKING TO YOUR AGELESS HEART

It is of importance to communicate with your heart. Even if you are young and think your heart is perfect, it is a good idea to encourage it and establish a conscious relationship. You don't have to be embarrassed about talking to yourself, children do it all the time. I speak to my heart as if it were a close friend, which it is. Of course, the best way to talk to your heart is by meditating on it. Just becoming still and centering your attention on your heart is the highest form of communication. Any time you feel tightness or squeezing in your chest, if you calmly and lovingly focus on your heart you will discover how much power over your body you actually have.

SIGHING

If you are thinking or straining too hard to come up with answers in your life, or you feel stuck in a place of emotional resistance, sighing is a wonderful technique to help you let go. By using the energy of sighing, you can turn your attention to that stillpoint of the heart that becomes a great expanse of nothingness into which your Higher Self can place the answers or the recognition of which direction to move.

One of the difficulties that causes stress to the heart is our perception that the answers to life must come immediately. We are so often on the treadmill of life, overreacting and overstimulated by the perpetual motion of our existence, that we forget how the truly wise choices and profound comprehension come from a timeless point of stillness in which the clarity of consciousness can recognize the hologram, can perceive the latticework and interconnection and relativity of all things.

You can teach your heart to relax and expand by giving it the command to "let go." It is very helpful to take a deep breath as you give this command and to **sigh**. As you exhale into the sigh, let everything you were holding be released in the sigh. In fact, the practice of sighing is a great way to relieve pressure in the heart. It is important to hear yourself make the sound of the sigh because it reminds you that the flow of energy is a releasing or outward flow. Make a series of sighs and as you sigh, simply command your body to relax so that it comes into a meditative state, then focus your attention within the space of your heart and chest and feel how different it feels.

SLEEP FOR THE HEART

Did you know that if you sleep on your left side, you may be putting too much pressure on your heart? This can be a problem if you habitually sleep on your left side to face or snuggle with your partner. It is worthwhile to discuss changing your sleeping habits so that neither of you are squeezing your heart. Try sleeping in the same direction on your right side, or on your back. Sleeping on your back is the most beneficial position for your body.

If you are feeling anxious, it is crucial to clear that fear before sleeping. What is in your consciousness before you sleep will emerge in the sleep state in an energetic form of dreaming that will influence your capacity to be peaceful in your life. Only a peaceful heart is an **ageless** heart. Sleep is one of the most important things you do because it allows the rebalancing of your physical and Emotional Body. How long you sleep is not nearly as important as how well you sleep. During sleep, the endocrine system repairs your cells and stress is washed from your body. You can teach yourself to sleep well and utilize sleep to revitalize your body. This is accomplished by removing all the residues of daily experience so that sleep is peaceful, rather than filled with the confusing dreams which are the Emotional Body's avenue of release. Here is how to do it:

Begin by spinning around before you sleep. As you spin in a clockwise direction, the stuck energy and even static electricity that so often causes insomnia, will be flung from the body, leaving it relaxed and clear. People who live in cities often suffer from insomnia simply because there is not enough earth around to drain away the static electricity that builds up in apartment buildings. Spinning releases negative energy and definitely brings about peaceful sleep and positive dreams. It also increases your immune system by quickening your vibration. Don't worry if you get dizzy after only a couple of turns. This is an indication of how much you need the spinning. Just spin until you feel a little dizzy and try to increase the number of turns by one each day.

Now, sit for a moment of meditation on your bed. You may also do this exercise lying down. Ask your body where it is holding any residue of fear. Wherever you feel a sensation or sense the place, bring your consciousness to that part of the body. Ask it what color it needs to dissolve the fear. Bring the color it chooses into that part of the body holding the fear. You can feel the change of your energy as the fear is released. You will wake up a stronger, happier person ready to meet the day.

This is a very important practice for the attainment of an **Ageless Body**, because if the body sleeps in peace, the actions of the pituitary, hypothalamus and pineal glands can bring renewed, rejuvenating and healing energy into the body.

LAUGHTER: SHAKING FREE

Laughter is one of the great remedies of the heart because it literally shakes, caresses and rocks the heart, causing it to let go. You have absolute control over your capacity to find laughter, to seek situations and experiences that bring laughter and allow you to express the child within. In truth, it is the child-like energies that keep you **ageless.**

When you laugh, the rhythm of the breath is changed. Breathing into the heart will alleviate its contraction and stress. The great purpose of the heart is to bring nutrients through the blood to every part of the body. That life-giving current comes with the deep and full breath which is always the finishing touch of heartfelt laughter.

Look around in your life for the people and situations that bring laughter to you. Sometimes pets are a great source of amusement, or the humor in books and movies. Try making the sound of laughter just to feel how it resonates in your chest. It doesn't even matter if you are pretending, it is the shaking that makes the difference. Laughter massages your heart and is absolutely the best exercise!

EXERCISE FOR THE AGELESS HEART

I remember one of my greatest anxieties about giving birth at forty-two was whether or not my heart would stand the strain. When the time came, I was mystified about how strong my heart felt. It seemed to like the effort of birthing and one of the greatest sensations in my body during and following the labor of birth was the feeling of strength in my heart. Never once did it flinch or palpitate; instead, my whole chest felt energized and extremely strong after the exertion. I knew that all the swimming and sand walking I had done during pregnancy had prepared me for the work of labor and I felt a great admiration for this wonderful muscle. My heart loved the exercise that allowed it to stretch out and perform its function to circulate the life-giving nutrients throughout my body and that of my baby.

Your heart was made for exercise, it loves to beat and bound as you give it a good workout. When you exercise your heart muscle, it clears away a great deal of the physiological debris caused by stress. Stress is caused by the congestion of energy, while exercise releases energy, as long as you do not overdo. When you exercise, the breath is increased and the oxygen feeds your body while the toxins are removed at the same time. Your body loves to move and you can find a thousand different ways to creatively stimulate your body. Though some people really love to "push" their body, exercise need not be hard or over- exerting. Just as laughter rocks and releases the entire chest, such things as dance, or even meandering, have a wonderful effect on the **ageless** heart because the motion brings pleasure and happy abandonment.

Spinning is a perfect exercise for the heart and the chest.

If you spin for only a few minutes, you will feel the lightness that comes into the chest and creates ever expanding arcs that fall from the heart down the arms into the hands. One of my daily exercises is to spin until I can feel the tingling charge coursing down my arms and out my hands. When I feel the tingle in my hands, I know my body is revitalized and charged with life and I feel ready to extend myself into the outside world.

WATER FOR THE AGELESS HEART

Have you ever focused on the sensations you feel when you are floating either face up or face down in water? Your breath cycle changes and you tend to take long sighing type breaths. It is a great gift to your heart to submerge your body in water. Laying in the water creates a weightless environment that takes the pressure off your heart and other inner organs. Even ten minutes in a weightless environment can bring you into a renewed state of tranquility. While swimming is an excellent exercise for the entire body, even floating in water is of great benefit in supporting and allowing the extension and relaxation to comfort and feed the heart. There is a subtle balancing that takes place when the fluids within the body and those around the body come into balance and resonance to each other.

THE HEART PROTECTOR

Did you know that around your heart is a liquid-filled sac called the pericardium? In Chinese medicine this protective membrane is called the heart protector. The fluid of the pericardium cushions the heart so that this great muscle can pump the blood undisturbed. I feel that the pericardium is crucial to health of the individual. Many times when I have looked psychically at a person, I have noted that the pericardium is congested and cloudy. This always means that the bio-chemical by-products of all their thoughts and feelings are congregating around the heart. I am convinced that the result of the squeezing that occurs when we are tense or angry charges the fluids of the pericardial sac with waste material caused by the alterations in the chemical balance of the pericardium. Very often when people have continual tension within the pericardium, they develop a sore spot behind the left scapula or shoulder blade. This spot is an actual acupuncture point the Chinese call "cure a hundred diseases" that radiates across the shoulder and around the heart. It corresponds to the brachial plexus nerve ganglion that radiates to the heart and down the arm.

All the "Window to the Sky" acupuncture points we activate in our work at The Light Institute circulate around through the pericardium and create a powerful energy which causes it to clear itself. These Windows anchor the celestial energies of higher consciousness into the body, which then can reach ecstatic states by transcending emotional stress.

WASHING YOUR HEART

One of the most powerful ways to keep your heart safe and strong to is meditate on the pericardium and keep its fluids clean and clear. Imagine that you can look inside your pericardium and actually see any residues that might stress your heart. If you find any dark spots or heavy areas, you can clear away this debris of physical or emotional blockage with the result of feeling lighter and more open again. It is a quite palpable sensation of lifting in the whole chest area as you wash away the negativity.

Visualize that you are flooding the pericardium with the most pristine, crystalline water that washes away all the cloudy particles and leaves it absolutely clear and rejuvenated. Let yourself experience your pericardium being filled with only the purest of light energy, inspirational feelings, ecstasy and joy.

MOVING YOUR HEART ENERGETICALLY

One of the side affects of my Mexico heart adventure was an annoying tendency towards irregular palpitation of my heart. Sometimes over-extension, or lack of physiological balances might cause momentary fibrillation of my heart. This is a strange sensation as if the heart were running away; it almost feels as if it were outside the body. Fibrillation is a dangerous occurrence and must be immediately stopped. I learned to employ acupressure techniques as well as stimulation to the heart meridian that would give me almost instantaneous relief. I want to pass these techniques on to you in case you can help someone who is troubled by pulse irregularity or any other difficulty. If the heart is passing a message indicating that it is having a momentary block, it is of great importance to answer that message with guidance and assurance so that what might have become a heart disorder can simply become a rebalancing homeostasis of energy.

Let me show you some acupuncture points that will help you release tension in your heart, so that this most important relationship, that of you and your own heart, becomes one of communication and understanding rather than fear and helplessness.

ACUPUNCTURE POINTS TO HELP YOUR HEART

The first point that helps my heart if it is beating irregularly is the acupuncture point called Shenmen (H. 7). It is a point of sedation which also moves the meridian, allowing the heart to reset itself. You can find this point on your own body and feel the rather strange electrical sensation, as if the nerves were going to sleep. By pressing into that point, the heart is able to rebalance itself.

Turn your hand palm upwards towards the ceiling and find the point in the indentation on the side of the wrist closest to your body. It is where the wrist articulates or moves from side to side. There is a tendon in that groove and if you place your thumbnail next to it and move your hand towards and away from your body, you will be able to feel when you have activated a sensation. It is a little like a tingling of a nerve. My heart stops fibrillating after only a few seconds. It is a good idea to stimulate this acupuncture point on a daily basis to keep the energies flowing.

There is another point that will nourish and rebalance your heart energies. This is called Shaochong (H 9) which is on the inside bottom quadrant of your nail on the little finger. It is the ending point of the heart meridian that begins under the armpit. Just grab hold of the end of your little finger and twist it as hard as you can for a few seconds to give it a good stimulation. If you have had congestion in your heart, you will notice that squeezing and twisting it feels tender. This is a good biofeedback technique to know how your heart energy is at any moment. As you twist your little finger every day you will notice that the tenderness recedes, because the heart is receiving the electromagnetic currents that flow through the acupuncture meridian.

In fact, not only is it a good idea to twist and squeeze your little finger on both hands, but twist all of your finger tips on both hands. Each contains acupuncture points that can rebalance and protect the energy flow of your body. The end of the middle finger is the point that effects the pericardium. It is very important to squeeze that finger as it will to help the pericardium to function. If for some reason you are having your fingers pricked to extract blood, I would recommend that you never the allow the technician to use that pericardium finger unless you feel that there is too much energy in the heart.

In Chinese medicine the nose is considered to be the organ of the heart and indeed, people with large emotional repertoires may have quite bulbous noses. Psychics, for

example, often have bulbous noses. Some people have a tendency towards nosebleeds. This is considered a message from the heart saying there is too much energy being bound and it is therefore rising back up out of the body. I have noticed this very often in children when nosebleeding becomes a phenomena related to too much excess emotion or energy such as too much competition in physical activity, for example. Chinese medicine has a very effective cure for nosebleeds which is pricking the outside of the thumb to bring the energy down and release congestion. Twisting the thumb will be of help in these situations and you can do it yourself!

Heart Acupuncture Points

SUPER-NUTRIENTS FOR THE AGELESS HEART

Although minute by minute biochemical and biomolecular researchers are coming up with new information about the body there are a few important new discoveries that have proven their effect on the heart. I want to share these super-nutrients with you because it is so wonderful to influence your heart with nurturing substances that correct imbalances and protect you from future difficulties.

COENZYME Q^{10}

Coenzyme Q^{10} was of great help to me after the damage to my heart in Mexico. Initially, I had the unpleasant experience of angina pectoral or chest pain. Searching for something other than a drug, I discovered coenzyme Q^{10} which solved the problem within only a few days.

Coenzyme Q^{10} has been studied around the world for its wonderful effect on the heart. Researchers in leading medical circles in Germany, Japan and recently the United States, have provided hundreds of papers demonstrating its value. Because it controls the flow of oxygen on the cellular level, it serves as a biochemical spark that supplies necessary energy. Coenzyme Q^{10} has been found to relieve hypertension and thus lower high blood pressure. Perhaps because it is such an excellent nutrient to the heart, it also stops palpitations which are sometimes caused by metabolic imbalances.

VITAMIN E

Vitamin E is not a new discovery. It has been used for over thirty years to help people with cardiovascular disease. It is so important to the heart that it must always be included in any discussion of heart nutrients. Vitamin E is a heart saver in several ways: It is a powerful fat soluble antioxidant that protects the heart from the damage done to cellular membranes from free radicals. It prevents clots, decreases the need for oxygen and thus helps relieve circulatory problems as well as supporting the heart in its functioning. Vitamin E increases stamina and is an important nutrient in any athletic regimen; however, if you suffer from high blood pressure, you should go slowly in its introduction to your system as it sometimes temporarily increases blood pressure. Usually intake is from 800 to 1200 I.U. units. I recommend that you talk to your nutritionist or doctor concerning appropriate dosage and form.

OROTATES AND BROMELAIN

These are the most exciting new heart helpers that may soon completely alter the way we apply the principals of cardiac prevention and care. They represent many years of scientific research and discovery as well as clinical application by one of the greatest medical giants of this century, Dr. Hans Nieper of Hanover, Germany. *

Dr. Nieper has discovered a way to deliver crucial nutrients to the specific areas of cardiac cells that prevent and protect them from invasion and at the same time keep them in an **ageless** state by providing the essentials for cellular metabolism.

Magnesium and potassium work to strengthen the heart muscle and can be delivered directly to the heart by a mineral carrier called orotate. Orotates have an affinity towards the heart, blood vessels, blood brain barrier and cartilage. Dr. Nieper utilized this affinity to insure that the magnesium and potassium could reach the specific heart cells through the chemical bonding with the orotates to form nutritional supplements of magnesium orotate and potassium orotate. Studies of thousands of people, both heart patients and healthy ones, show that the supplementation of these natural nutrients reduce heart attacks to an almost negligible level.

BROMELAIN

Bromelain is an enzyme extracted from the stems of pineapples. It acts as a veritable pipe cleaner for coronary arteries and vessels. Through its cleaning action, bromelain prevents the narrowing of the arteries of the heart which otherwise could lead to heart attacks. An important attribute of Bromelain is its ability to dissolve fibrin clots and inhibit platelet aggregation. You may not realize how important this fact is to you until you know that your computer, TV, and even your hairdryer cause clumping of blood cells. Toxins, and especially **tap water** clump the blood cells in such a way as to damage their capacity to carry oxygen and nutrients. This is why you feel tired so often!

Dr. Nieper suggests a formula of Magnesium orotate, 1500-2500 mg/day, Potassium orotate 150-300 mg daily, and Bromelain 120-140 mg daily. *

L CARNITINE

Your heart muscle, unlike skeletal muscle, uses fatty acids rather than glucose for fuel and energy force. Cardiac muscle is dependent upon carnitine, a substance found naturally in the body, to facilitate the burning of these long-chain fatty acids. The difficulty is that sometimes there is insufficient carnitine produced and the fatty acids cannot get across the cellular membranes into the extra-mitochondrial matrix to provide the fuel for the heart muscle to have a strong and regular beat. Carnitine is abundant in fish, sheep muscle and avocados. Carnitine ferries the fatty acids across the membranes and into the right place, then stimulates their oxidation so that the heart can receive the energy it needs to function.

One of the most shocking recent discoveries relating to the dreaded cardiac infarction increase in industrialized nations is the correlation between the use of ionic polyglycols (dishwasher detergents) and the incidence of cardiac infarction! The polyglycols seem to interfere with fatty acid combustion by the heart, which then renders it helpless to perform its task. This has been documented by Dr. Nieper as well as Dr. Wildenthal of the University of Texas at Dallas. It is quite sobering to contemplate the effect of the many thousands of environmental toxins on the intricate metabolism of our bodies. We must counteract them with all the protection we can muster both from nutritional support as well as the power of our energetic relationship with our bodies!

BECOME FRIENDS WITH YOUR HEART

Your heart is your friend. You can teach it to become **ageless** by creating an open dialog in which it can communicate with you about what is going on so that you can direct the energetic changes that help it to stay vital and young. Energy is the language of your heart and you can teach yourself to master the conscious directive of that energy. Through the heart comes the resolution to any dilemma, whether it is one of emotions or physical vitality. If you circle positive, peaceful energy around and through the pericardium and the heart, all its fear will subside and it will return to its natural state of perfection.

PEACE AND THE AGELESS HEART

The final mandate of the **ageless heart** is the peace to beat its eternal rhythm and set the pace for a healthy, fulfilling life. The secret of peace is the recognition of the Higher Self. The more you explore yourself, the less reactive you will be in your life and the steadier will be your heart as it responds calmly to incoming stimuli. As you teach yourself to view all experiences as gifts for growth, you will find the inner strength to face all situations with peace in your heart, for your life is truly your own!

** If you are concerned about your heart, I highly recommend reading Dr. Nieper's **Revolution in Technology, Medicine and Society**.*

LETTING GO OF DEATH: THE ULTIMATE TRANSCENDENCE

"Death can be met without aging. These two things, aging and death, are not inextricable partners."

You might think it odd to end this book on the **Ageless Body** with a chapter about death, but you cannot know life until you have dismissed death as the illusion it truly is. Though it is very likely that death will be conquered in the near future, that will never occur because we wish to avoid it and are clutching at our physical bodies. If we are to become **ageless** beings, capable of wandering the universe indefinitely, it will be because we will have learned to love and honor physical form as an expression of our infinite Soul. We will have mastered the capacity to move in the Light Body, performing the miraculous feats of those whose legacy we have become; not because it has been given to us, but because we will have sought out the knowings that have been awaiting the advancement of our collective consciousness for thousands of years. What was once the solemn secret of the few will belong to all who open the window of enlightenment and allow the knowing to flood their bodies. You and I have the right to use our bodies for as long as we desire, to build and rebuild them as we choose, and finally to leave them when we are ready to go on up the evolutionary ladder. That is the blueprint prepared by our Soul, and we have the power to use it in exactly that way.

Humanity will never experience what the masters have demonstrated of long lifespans, until the lurking shadow of the fear of death is released from within the DNA. You must find that archaic thought-form and ferret it out of your being. It has become embedded in you along with all the other psychic and genetic material you inherited from your relatives, as well as from the accumulation of memories from previous memories that are stored in the mind of the cell. The challenge is not to be healthy to avoid death, but to be **ageless** through the pure joy of existence. You become **ageless** as your consciousness embraces and recognizes your Light Body in its multidimensional capacity to be nourished and fed from the energies of the cosmos. Embodiment is not a burden of separation, but rather a vehicle of communication that transcends any particular dimension or position. It continually brings you face to face with a timeless present, dedicated to learning and giving the gifts that your body so gladly supplies the world.

This command over the body can only be utilized if you are willing to explore the essence energies that compose the body on subtle and sub-atomic levels. You can not abuse your body with negativity (physical, emotional or mental) and hope to not age and die. If you seek immortality because you think your present body must be preserved and fear being lifted away from it, you will not attain mastery because your motive stems from fear. People often pray for immortality because they think they must be perpetually the same. You cannot remain the same for more than a moment; a major law of energy is motion and change. The **ageless body** is not a form of denial or refusal to follow natural law, it is an invitation to practice manifestation on the level of creation which necessitates the awareness of cosmic law as it moves into and through the physical realms.

You must grapple with your fear if you are to attain this breakthrough. Fear ravages the body, pinching its lifeline of pathways, nerves, muscles and organs. As I have laid out numerous ways to embrace the **Ageless Body**, I must also include this conversation about death, so that you can assimilate its teaching and return to the magnificent potential of life!

FEAR OF DEATH

We admire and seek youth because we fear death. We propel ourselves into the material world to avoid the whispers of an internal reality that portends our undeniable future. Even a low profile, a life of nebulous accomplishment or feeling, seems preferable to the subtle threat of nonexistence. Yet all the avoidance techniques we devise cannot keep us from the rush of the ongoing energies that will one day, inevitably, carry us back across the threshold of this world, into the source from which we came. That drive to come to the end is not one that demands the desecration or aging of the body; to the contrary, it is the lack of living that deteriorates the will and saps the spirit, and which motivates the body to continue on towards death.

Our bodies carry the memories of all those who have gone before us, including their deaths. These memories are indelibly written within the genetic makeup of our species. After death, consciousness disengages from the body which can no longer experience or relay what happens beyond the mystical separation of the two, leaving future generations caught without an ending to the play. We must now diligently reach out to retrieve the threads of life from wherever they have gone, and in so doing discover what the masters have told us all along: "There is no death."

In truth, there is no end nor beginning to the life force energies that so illicitly slip through the veils of the manifest and unmanifest worlds. The bodies we inhabit have always been impregnated with the memories of other incarnations so that even the tiny new baby is but an old soul in a freshly woven cloak. When the soul has played the game and placed the last piece into the puzzle, the body will know its time has come, and will begin to unravel its fabric so to be woven once again.

Though science contends that human genes will allow a maximum of 115 years, there is no proof that aging is a part of any death program designed by genes. It would seem more likely that aging is a habit of humans who have forgotten how to continue physical perfection on the cellular level.

Death can be met without aging. These two things: aging and death, are not inextricable partners. It has been our illusion that aging is the cruel game of death, playing with our bodies like the cat with the proverbial mouse. We must realize that death is a natural process and therefore need not be the culmination of neglect or the general deficit of life force. Ultimately, death need not be from age or disease, but rather a harmonious function of the soul's purpose. Let us explore this in-depth aspect of death as a part of sacred life.

DEATH AS AN INITIATION

For eons of time, the family of humanity has been carrying deep within its genes a thought-form which whispers to the body that death must be avoided, that it is painful, and we must turn our face away from death to avoid any nuance of its presence or its teaching. But death is the greatest teacher of all. It is an energetic process, a funnel of initiation that transports us from one state of consciousness to another. Our fear of death keeps us from really embracing life because we encumber ourselves with the illusion and burden of caution, as if it were a mighty armor against a crafty invader. Not so!

Death itself is not painful; death is an experience of light. Death bestows upon us the kiss of freedom and the direction towards home. We need not seek it as it comes on its own, but we must regard it with more dignity and imbue it with purpose that helps us to put it in its place, rather than allowing the fear of it to usurp the energies of our lives.

Death is not merely a translation or passage from one state to another; it is an energy of transcendence -- the actual vehicle that carries the body not only across, but up to higher levels of existence. Jesus the Christ tried to demonstrate this to us, but we were too dense and heavy in our physical bodies to follow his light. The morbid and doubtful modern man seems even more unable to break free enough from his negativity to contemplate the reality of an "afterlife." The smallest child has experienced consciousness outside of his tiny body, yet why do we find it so difficult to recognize or remember that our body is but one facet of our true self? The **Ageless Body** is based on this elementary knowing.

PRACTICING DEATH

Death is something that we must not only remember and look at directly, but that we must practice, so that in each moment we recognize how we can come to the point of energetic translation without fear. We can experience the great love of recognition about the perfect moment of any death, whether it is on the level of cell, or the level of the entire body. Dying is really the art of transcendence.

If you will allow yourself to practice the passage of transcendence, you will live your life in a completely different way. With that burst of free energy at the moment of death, there is a transcendence which transmutes it into something of a higher vibration. The energy is still living and present; it is simply transcended into dimensions beyond those that we recognize in our physical bodies. It is not beyond the reach of our understanding because every person has the memory of consciousness beyond body.

Everyone of us, at least once in our lives has had experiences of flying or being out of body and looking down at it, even if you don't consciously remember it. Perhaps as a child you had the proverbial nightmare in which you were flying or falling. You thought you were dreaming, although you probably remember how real it felt to your body. Through this experience, your consciousness took some part of your body beyond this world.

When old people daydream in the sun, their cellular memory is activated by those other octaves that carry them home to the light. Old people and children have difficulty in translating those energetic realities into vocabularies that we can understand, and yet we, ourselves, are not barred from having these same experiences. Through them we can begin to directly know death as a passage to another plain of existence.

Years ago I was directed to make a cassette tape on death. It is called *Death and Samadhi*. In the end I give an exercise I have used a great deal with terminally ill people and their families. The person creates an avenue of white light and either steps onto it themselves, or helps another to do so. It is a moving light, like an escalator that carries them upward into the heavens. If there is great fear, I suggest that they concentrate on the feeling of love coming towards them from others they know who have gone before them. This is very soothing because they need to find a point of reference in this unremembered world from which they came into body.

HOW THE LIGHT INSTITUTE WORKS WITH DEATH

At the Light Institute, we help people to experience and release their hidden fears and memories of death within a multi-incarnational context. The work has a profound effect on one's ability to face life. It gives the body a chance to divest itself from old residues that poison its potential for living.

When we are working on people to clear deaths, we want to help them release those fears and memories that are blocking their life force energy in this present life. If the physical body has no range of motion, if it is afraid to ride the bicycle, step on the ladder, or swim in the water, then so goes the life! The overriding biological message from the body is, "Be careful, watch out." It will take over any emotional desire for ecstasy. If the body is carrying imprints of its imminent death or memories of death it has experienced before, these factors will inhibit life. So it is very important to teach people to embrace death consciously, to explore it as they would explore the different colors of flowers in a garden. We need to learn that we have had so many deaths that each death has taught the body something. By releasing that death, we release ourselves to life.

If a person has experienced a traumatic death in another lifetime, it will influence the way the person develops. If someone has a theme of holding hurt in their heart or not speaking the truth, they will have played those themes out physically in the lifetimes. In other words, they will re-experience lifetimes in which they have been strangled, in which that part of the physical body, the heart or throat, which represents the theme they are working on, has been physically damaged or destroyed. We must dissolve that blocked memory so that the theme can come forward and be released from the body. By allowing the physical body to express the thematic experience, we are affecting the capacity to do it on our emotional and spiritual levels -- they are all swirling together.

The physical body is the first body to hold the imprint of a soul lesson because it carries "the brunt of the spirit," expressing physically what the soul is working on spiritually. The facilitator might ask the body to bring forth the memory of death that is holding the person back from life now. From this we will garner the theme that is causing the blockage. Perhaps it has to do with communication, or sexual energy, or the fear of moving forward. By letting the body pick the life or death that it wants to release, it will tell us what is happening now in the hidden recesses of the Emotional Body.

On some levels the most dangerous thing about death is our mental fascination with it. The mind loves to spin the death theme and imagine it mentally in many different ways. This is why people love murder mysteries, sensational news stories, and killer-thriller movies. It is not that they necessarily feel anything by seeing the blood and gore on the film, but it is because of the shockwave it creates in the mind. The mind is conceptualizing and practicing the idea -- the idea of death.

We are unbalanced by the mind's idea of death because we have not attained the recognition of it as a spiritual transcendence; we have not experienced death in its full cycle. We have not been able to take the concept of death and carry it through the experience so that we see the outcome. We are caught at the mental level. If we could realize that we already know death, we would deal with it much differently. We have separated from death experientially in the Western world, creating a safe distance from it by leaving it to those who will take responsibility. Because we have disconnected from it, it has become exciting to us as a concept. What we do not experience looms large for us because we "think" about it, and then we create it in our lives.

The unconscious and conscious aspects of the mind begin to play back and forth with each other. If the conscious mind holds death conceptually, the unconscious mind begins to design it. That design creates an electromagnetic charge. The Emotional Body recognizes that charge and seeks it by viewing a movie or reading a book which explores the death theme. It is practicing death on an energetic level. By so doing, it creates an energy that is loose in the universe of the physical body and begins to imprint the mind of the cell to prepare for its death.

Little children, about the age of five, become aware of death. Five, six and seven year-olds are quite often fascinated by the possibility of dying. It is interesting to note that from about four years of age, children begin to spontaneously remember other incarnations. This is most likely the reason they awaken to the memory of death. At puberty, the actual capacity for immortality begins when the master glands stimulate the gonads to reproduce life, thus perpetuating its natural progression.

Science is investigating the possibility of a "death hormone" that may be initiated at the time of puberty when the body realizes the capacity to reproduce itself. The advent of sexual maturity may trigger the subtle dying process because the body has potentially fulfilled its biological purpose. Perhaps, in reality, we are no different than the wild flower!

This is why teenagers so often have very strong feelings that "I will only live until I am 30," or "I know I will die young." They start perceiving the actions set in motion by these subtle energies of death, the imminence of death, which, of course, has been going on from the beginning of birth as cells are born, mature and die. There is a concentration of energy which causes the consciousness to be impregnated with the reality of it. The mental focus on death designs most of the death on this planet. The moment there is a window for the potential of death, we often take it. We have already fantasized about it emotionally.

A common thought-form of children is, "I'll just die and then you'll be sorry." "If I weren't here, you would miss me," or "I'll die if you don't love me", or even " I wish you would die!" It begins in childhood, echoes into the teens and on into adulthood. The difficulty is that once the Emotional Body gets hold of this power and feels that it can be used over others, it realizes that this is one of the biggest weapons ever invented. The threat of death provides the illusion that one has the final word other another. The passion of its potential sets in motion a probable reality that will ultimately carry itself out. All of the judgment and self-hatred begin to produce the symptoms of death.

Illness is a symptom of death. Once the body begins to have the experience of becoming ill and practicing death, it repeats itself. People develop chronic diseases as an expression of the hidden urge to die and let go of the struggle to live. It is important to recognize that once the mind incorporates death, it inevitably begins to design the process that ultimately moves with its own volition. The consciousness begins to move into the mental/emotional arena whereby the mind stimulates the emotional imprint that effects the physical vehicle. Opportunities are then formed through life, accidents and illness, whereby we have a conscious choice to die.

I remember one such choice I had in Galisteo. I was galloping home from a wonderful afternoon, riding my horse across the plains. Just before we reached the gates, my white horse, Girl, suddenly shied to one side. Riding bareback, I had no saddle to protect me from the lurch. I will never forget the sensation as I slid over her right shoulder and onto my back on the ground. I felt the ripples of her muscles as she extended her leg and the heat of her body, but I didn't feel the ground at all. Lying there in utter vulnerability, I watched with great fascination as her thundering hoofs began to descend toward my head. I actually weighed the choice to live or die at that moment. First my mind said, "yes, now," and then I quietly responded "no" to myself just as her hoof hit the ground a tiny fraction of an inch from my head.

The entire scene was played out in slow motion while my sensory body took in every detail. I noticed the striations on her hoof and the soft frog at the back of it, and especially the way the air molecules parted as she brought her foot down. Though I felt absolutely no fear, I was extremely lucid. I felt her panic as she realized she might step on me. I lay there for quite awhile and witnessed the experience, replaying itself over and over in my mind. I was acutely aware that the choice had been mine. If I had stayed with the "yes," I would have been dead.

After that, Girl and I developed a very close psychic connection. I would give her the rein and she would charge across the plains at full gallop, dodging cactus and leaping arroyos, but I never fell off again. I don't think she would have let me. We were partners in that episode and she did not want it to happen again as I had frightened her more than myself!

The mental fear of dying causes much of the pain sensations that often plague people before the final stage of death. Anxiety causes contraction, which results in increased pain. Often the emotional resistance includes both an attraction and repulsion at the same time.

Death is not simultaneous, it is a closing down. The physical body is transmuted and the life force energy transcends its physical body and is taken up the Spiritual Body. People have always described death as a shadow that comes and hovers, but it is really the sense of darkness on the cellular level as the light is driven from the cells in their dying process. The shadow is actually the threshold to the light. As it opens, death welcomes us home to the conscious embrace of our Spiritual Body.

The Spiritual Body is beyond the range of emotional fear or physical expression and comes in to bring about new experiences that occur during, or actually after, the process of dying has been completed. There is a burst of light that completes the transmutation.

When the Light Institute works with people, we are interested in focusing our attention on death as a spiritual experience. How does the Spiritual Body embrace death?

In order for there to be growth on earth, we must be able to move past the point of physical death and make clear contact with the spiritual experience that releases us from the memories in the body. If we can begin to do this, people will be born who are not afraid of death and who will be able to go into the Light Body. One of the things that holds us away from the Light Body is the trigger that so much light in the body is a reminder of death. As we teach people to become aware of this, we can actually influence the kind of dying that takes place on this planet. If somebody sees that they must return to their source, they can leave the body with choice of will and grace.

GRACE AND WILL

Do you know that prayer, "Now I lay me down to sleep, I pray the Lord my soul to keep. If I should die before I wake, I pray the Lord my soul to take?"

I said that prayer every night when I was a child. It always created a certain kind of anxiety; not only the anxiety about whether I would be taken, but the anxiety of the " before I wake," which imprinted a fear of having it done "to" me. It implied that there was a possibility I would die without knowing it. This set up a conscious mental and emotional threshold of surrender through which I passed every night when I said the prayer. I felt that I died each night and would awaken in the morning a bit surprised that I was still here. The effect of the prayer created an activation of my will to live, as well as my will to die.

It is important to practice the will of dying with grace, not the will to die in order to avoid life because you feel that you cannot survive. You must practice the will to live, until you know you have transcended the illusions of life. It cannot be because the ego is afraid of death, but because your soul is teaching you about the connection between the two.

There is a Native American expression which says: "This is a good day to die!" It speaks of a philosophy in which the body surrenders to the Great Spirit. It does what it must do with dignity, without resistance. It is not the surrender of depression or disconnection from purpose, neither is it morbidity or lack of will; rather it is as if you were reaching up, as if you were already beaming light, willing to transcend and let go of the crystallized form of yourself entrapped in body. Your body will not resist transcendence into light because it is comfortable in its memory of the experience. You have done it before.

When you surrender to the Spiritual Body, it will lift you up to a frequency where you are aware that your will is connected to something which is bigger. That "something" is your spiritual destiny.

PEACEFUL DEATH

In truth we have died a thousand deaths. Somewhere within us is the recognition, the memory that we have been able to lift from our body into a state of grace, without suffering, pain or fear, simply pronouncing that it is enough, and either leaving our body or taking it with us into the energetic frequencies that are our source. If we are in touch with our Spiritual Body, we can remember these choices and the peace with which we have transcended physical form.

At the Light Institute, we place great emphasis on the body remembering its capacity to die in peace. Such memories help people to release fear and become more peaceful in their lives. In the Western world, we have been taught resistance as a way of survival which removes us from any and almost all proximity to the energy of true peace. It is time for us to return to the sense of safety and adventure that helps us to discover new ways of living that are in harmony with natural laws.

Without resistance, we can experience ourselves being pushed through the funnel of initiation, across the veil into a different octave. If we can encourage the body to process itself normally so that the dying cells die and the new ones are born, we can be in perfect resonance with the natural pulse of the body; Birth, Death, Birth, Death. There is a release of energy in the cell that dies, and a burst of energy as a new one is born.

Within our bodies right now, thousands of cells are dying. They are dying in accordance with their own time-clock, or dying because of the stress and pollution of the internal environment. If we can imagine, or allow ourselves to feel, the process of the dying of any one of those cells, we will come to the point where that dying cell disintegrates. Its materializing no longer serves the whole and so it is released back into pure energy which stimulates the birth of its daughter-cell. Peaceful death is attainable when we experience the reality that we never cease to exist, we simply change the form and expression of our consciousness!

RENEWAL

Renewal is something your body knows how to accomplish. Every seven years of your life, within the span, all the cells of your body, except those of your brain and heart muscle, are exchanged for new cells. You literally have a new body every seven years and your body does it without resistance, continually opening to new energy. If you practice all the teachings and exercises in this book -- speaking to your heart, nourishing your endocrine system, viewing the quality of your fluids -- you will be well on your way to the **Ageless Body**. The quickening of your vibratory energy will lift you onto octaves of consciousness in which freedom and choice are always available to you.

DEATH RELEASES LIGHT

At the moment we lift up from the body, there is an overpowering explosion of light as the body transcends physical form and returns to the energies of Light Body. We are made of light. The DNA whispers its perfect code to our **Ageless Body**, passing from one cell to another, this translation of information surrounded by ultraviolet light in the fluid medium of its carrier. So, too, is death encompassed by unlimited light.

In all the stories of the great books, in the various religions and even in the transmissions that have been passed to humanity from other dimensions, the message is always about the Light Body.

In the Bible and other books, certainly in civilizations that we have heard of from other planets, are the stories of those who live in the **ageless** state of perfect embodiment. Their lifespan is greatly extended from the lifespan of our own and they seem to be unconcerned that death can choose them without their conscious direction or mandate. There are beings who have not aged at all and whose bodies have been present upon our planet for 800 years and more.

This is because the atomic structure of the cell is within resonance to the DNA, so that the body's sense of itself is the very sense of life. We have heard of the miracles of saints and great masters who levitated, bi-located, and have lived **ageless**ly. As they appear from one place to another, they appear in vehicles of light or in their own radiant Light Bodies. There are accounts of seeing them as if one could look through them, or seeing them with the halos of light that simply are the confirmation of the vibratory level that they are utilizing within their perpetual state of **ageless**ness.

The light radiance they demonstrate should encourage us to explore the profound connection between light and life.

I remember one of the true stories of such a beautiful death that has stayed with me throughout my life. It is the story of the death of Yogananda, a great master of the East, who upon dying, left his body in a perfect, harmonic state in which the cells did not putrify. There was no disturbance or disintegration to his body because it was already in a perfect state of light. How did he do that? He did it through his perfect love, through his profound communication with **every** cell of his body. Any cell that was in the dying phase was released into light and all his cells were embraced by his divinity.

You too, can experience your own Light Body. You can do this first by going to the level of the atom of the cell and communicating with that energy. At this level, you can view your body and perceive the source of life as it lives within the trillions of cells of your physical being. You must be willing to extend the mandate, so that your cells can model this body of light.

THE END WITHOUT AN END

The search for your **Ageless Body** will carry you beyond the limits of what you perceive as reality, into breathtaking panoramas of human potential. You must take this journey only with the joy of discovery and not with the anxiety of need. If you give your cells a mental command of health, you must also give it an energetically felt force of motion to carry out the mandate. You have the tools now to wield your body to a peaceful and fully conscious level in concert with the laws of energy. The very fact that you have discovered a true form of communication with your body will enhance your life immeasurably!

As you strengthen that direct relationship with your body, let yourself enjoy the fantastic benefits and rewards it offers you both. If you want to be more physical, just image yourself with all the feelings and sensations that correspond to the action and your body will effortlessly follow suit. Always remember to thank your body for each thing it accomplishes, just as you would another person. Indeed, it is a person, with its own specific needs and forms of expression. Your body must be honored as the great friend and teacher it is to you. It is your lifelong companion who unlocks the key to your own evolutionary spiral, set in motion by your soul.

Your willingness to explore timeless reality is of great benefit to all of humankind. As you discover sub-atomic divine life energy, you are releasing that force into the human atmosphere where others can perceive it and so begin their own search for the **Ageless Body**. Can you imagine what will happen to the habit of daily life when humanity realizes that there is no hurry because everything actually happens at once? We do not have to struggle to rush from one thing to another, hoping to find the time to get everything done. We must conceive of and design all that needs to take place within the hologram of interconnectedness, in which each thing is associated to everything else. We can set it all in motion by focusing in any one place and perceiving all its points of association. The laws of manifestation are not a linear force, but a holographic pulsation of energies that congregate to the center and then move out again in waves of energy that form third-dimensional reality.

The perfect place to practice holographic consciousness is in your physical body. For example, as you glance at the endocrine chart and ask which gland needs your attention, you will discover that after a few weeks of practice, you will begin to perceive them all at once, and you will be able to not only able tell which ones need your attention, but will actually feed them all simultaneously! The same is true of the body's fluids. You can look at those in your pericardium as the point of reference, and then spread your surveillance out through all the fluid systems of the body and perceive them all in one moment of conscious awareness.

Work patiently and lovingly with your body and you will feel the results of your commitment in a very short time. No matter your age, your body will respond to direct communication with you in a form that will forever change not only your physical energies, but your profound sense of yourself as well. What a magnificent awakening to discover that this body you have been ignoring or trying to get out of, turns out to be the vehicle of cosmic energy to which you were unconsciously trying to return!

At any moment you can transmute your negative images of yourself and replace them with the experience of glowing vibrancy that is the hallmark of the **Ageless Body.** It is a state of being that radiates the light of perfect love for all that is. It is your right and your destiny to claim your own **Ageless Body.**

The work contained in this book is taught at:
The Light Institute
HC-75, Box 50
Galisteo, New Mexico 87540
USA
Phone 505-983-1975
Fax 505-989-7217

466 1975 4336 Volunteer

The Nizhoni School for Global Consciousness
Route 14, Box 203
Santa Fe, (La Cienega), NM 87505
USA

For information in Europe please contact:
The Light Institute of Europe
Boîte Postale 6
F-16390 St. Sévérin, Frankreich

Phone: 003 45 98 0721
Fax: 003 45 98 9203

Chris Griscom is also the author of:
Time is an Illusion
Ecstasy is a New Frequency
The Healing of Emotion
Leben ist Liebe (Life is Love)
Feminine Fusion
Ocean Born: Birth as Initiation
Nizhoni: The Higher Self in Education

The following tapes are available at The Light Institute:
Audio Tapes
The Dance of Relationship
Parent Child Relationships
Death and Samadhi
Knowings
The Creative Self
Desert Trilogy: Healing, Sexuality and Radiation

Video Tapes
Windows to the Sky: Light Institute Exercises with
    Chris Griscom
Windows to the Sky: Connecting with Invisible Worlds
The Ageless Body

SUGGESTED READING

Chang, Steven T. - *The Complete System of Self Healing, Internal Exercises* (The Turtle Neck Exercises, pg. 113-119) Tao Publishing, 1986

Da Lin - *Taoist Health Exercise Book*, New York: The Putnam Publishing Group, 1983 (also published in German)

Haroldine - *Lithium and Lithium Crystals, Nature in Harmony*, Carberville, CA: Borderland Science Reserach Foundation, 1988

Lauffer, John - *Waterwise*, 5 Caswallen Drive, West Chester, PA 19380

Kelder, Peter - *Ancient Secret of the "Foundation of Youth,"* Revised Ed., Washington: Harbor Press, 1985 (published in German)

Nieper, Hans A. - *Revolution in Technology Medicine and Society, Conversation of Gravity Field Energy*, Oldenburg, Germany: MIT Verlag, 1981

Pearson and Shaw, Sandy and Durk - *Life Extension, a Practical Scientific Approach*, New York: Warner Books, 1982

Schechter, Steven R. - *Fighting Radiation & Chemical Pollutants with Foods, Herbs & Vitamins*, Encinitas, CA: Vitality, Inc., 1990